yourself

the clinton factor

the clinton factor
communicating
with charisma

dave gillespie and mark warren

Launched in 1938, the **teach yourself** series grew rapidly in response to the world's wartime needs. Loved and trusted by over 50 million readers, the series has continued to respond to society's changing interests and passions and now, 70 years on, includes over 500 titles, from Arabic and Beekeeping to Yoga and Zulu. What would you like to learn?

be where you want to be with **teach yourself**

For UK order enquiries: please contact Bookpoint Ltd, 130 Milton Park, Abingdon, Oxon OX14 4SB. Telephone: +44 (0) 1235 827720. Fax: +44 (0) 1235 400454. Lines are open 09.00–17.00, Monday to Saturday, with a 24-hour message answering service. Details about our titles and how to order are available at www.teachyourself.co.uk

For USA order enquiries: please contact McGraw-Hill Customer Services, PO Box 545, Blacklick, OH 43004-0545, USA. Telephone: 1-800-722-4726. Fax: 1-614-755-5645.

For Canada order enquiries: please contact McGraw-Hill Ryerson Ltd, 300 Water St, Whitby, Ontario L1N 9B6, Canada. Telephone: 905 430 5000. Fax: 905 430 5020.

Long renowned as the authoritative source for self-guided learning – with more than 50 million copies sold worldwide – the **teach yourself** series includes over 500 titles in the fields of languages, crafts, hobbies, business, computing and education.

British Library Cataloguing in Publication Data: a catalogue record for this title is available from the British Library.

Library of Congress Catalog Card Number: on file.

First published in UK 2008 by Hodder Education, part of Hachette Livre UK, 338 Euston Road, London, NW1 3BH.

First published in US 2008 by The McGraw-Hill Companies, Inc.

This edition published 2008.

The **teach yourself** name is a registered trade mark of Hodder Headline.

Typeset by Transet Limited, Coventry, England.
Printed in Great Britain for Hodder Education, an Hachette Livre UK Company, 338 Euston Road, London NW1 3BH, by CPI Cox & Wyman, Reading, Berkshire RG1 8EX.

The publisher has used its best endeavours to ensure that the URLs for external websites referred to in this book are correct and active at the time of going to press. However, the publisher and the author have no responsibility for the websites and can make no guarantee that a site will remain live or that the content will remain relevant, decent or appropriate.

Hachette Livre UK's policy is to use papers that are natural, renewable and recyclable products and made from wood grown in sustainable forests. The logging and manufacturing processes are expected to conform to the environmental regulations of the country of origin.

Impression number   10 9 8 7 6 5 4 3 2 1
Year   2012 2011 2010 2009 2008

contents

foreword

By Chris Cramer, Former President, CNN International

I am sure many of us have been there and I'm not sure that either time or advanced age is a great healer.

I refer to the sheer terror caused by an impending speech, a presentation to colleagues or clients , a wedding speech as Best Man or Friend of the Bride, or – much worse – an oration delivered at a funeral in honour of departed loved ones.

They say that public speaking is our number one fear. The sleepless nights, the days of anguish, the body sweats just before we reach the podium. I had a friend who frequently vomited before he took the stage. I myself have fainted at least twice waiting in the wings. And let's not forget those poor souls who have resorted, on occasions, to 'fight or flight' prescription drugs to get them through the ordeal.

On the other hand, there are those who appear effortless as they address the world. Those brilliant public speakers who are able to stride purposefully to the podium, remove a single sheet of paper from their pockets, smile broadly and, within minutes, have us eating out of their hands. We are entranced by their eloquence. In awe of their oratory.

Life can seem so unfair.

This book lifts the lid on the art of public speaking, of brilliant communication. It does so by focusing on former US President, Bill Clinton, while at the same time reminding us of the best communicators of our time; Sir Winston Churchill, Martin Luther King, President John F Kennedy, Nelson

Mandela, and one of my favourites, Colonel Tim Collins, of the Royal Irish Regiment, who sent his men into battle in Iraq in 2003 with the kind of speech that you imagine Julius Caesar gave his Roman legions. The kind of speech that chills your spine and lifts your soul.

This is not a book for those in love with PowerPoint or for those who believe that talking in public is all about reading the words on the screen while the rest of us watch the clock and pray for the session to end before we shoot ourselves. It is about taking the skills and expertise we may have and translating them into a narrative – a story – that other people might care to listen to. It's about one of the most brilliant communicators of our time who, whether you care much or little about his politics, has the gift of charisma and eloquence that anyone who wishes to speak in public should aspire to.

It reminds us early on that the best communicators edit their presentations and edit them again, and then again. So let me do so.

This is a great book. Keep reading.

foreword

By Jeremy Thompson, Sky News Presenter

Excellent communications skills are the essence of television news. First comes the tale, then the tell. Content is King, but delivery is the Household Cavalry. It always helps to have a good story. But the key is how you get it over to people. An audience won't listen unless you're engaging, accessible, compelling and credible.

In over 30 years in TV I've seen all the latest fancy technology, new gizmos, clever graphics and glitzy studios. Not once, but many times repeated. In the end it all comes down to having a damn good yarn, looking the viewers in the eye and telling them a story they can't turn off. News hasn't changed that much since the times when town criers strode in the main square armed with no more than a bell, a strong voice and a way with words. It always has been down to the way you tell it.

Politicians aren't much different when it comes to marketing policies, persuading voters and selling dreams. Bill Clinton is the best I've ever seen. Watching him in action you knew he was born to be President. As Chief US Correspondent for Sky News in the mid 1990s, I reported on Clinton in his Washington heyday. I soon realized he was the consummate communicator. He could grab and hold your attention from two feet to 200 yards and, through television, up to 20,000 miles. He just had *it*. The ability to capture your attention, hold you in his sway, lead you on a journey of ideas with his words, make you believe and leave you feeling you still wanted more. He had the skill to make everyone feel that they were the only one he was speaking to when he talked – whether they were face-to-face or they were part of a vast campaign throng. I've talked to battle-hardened TV news veterans, sceptical of his legendary charms, who admitted going weak at the knees when they were finally confronted by Bubba Bill.

I remember one particular day in Detroit during the 1996 Election Campaign when Clinton flew into town and addressed meeting after meeting. First it was the toughest of all blue-collar crowds on the shop floor of a car plant, who were soon cheering for Bill. Then it was onto a gathering of religious leaders of different faiths. Within minutes they were captivated and enthralled. Next, the city's captains of industry – more Republican than Democrat – but soon buying the party line. Finally it was a vast town hall meeting packed with regular voters, quickly beguiled by The Clinton Factor. In between he spoke to every small child, old lady and passing punter like he was their best pal. An extraordinary masterclass in communicating. As always, he had almost everyone rapt, spellbound, buying into Bill's message. It was like he tapped into the mains when he walked into a room and became energized by the power of the people within it. It was all about the way he used his words, wove his stories, altered his tone and changed the mood. Part-politician, part-preacher, part-storyteller but above all a brilliant communicator.

By examining the various facets of Bill Clinton's charisma, delivery and all-round performance, *Teach Yourself The Clinton Factor* makes the components of great communication accessible to us all.

The actor, David Gillespie, and writer, Mark Warren, have many acting and writing credits between them in TV, film and stage. They are also partners in The Speechworks, which specializes in one-to-one presentation skills training for public figures, sports personalities, board directors and senior executives.

Acknowledgements

The authors would like to thank the following for their invaluable help and assistance: Jill Birch, Liz Earle, Alison Frecknall, Dan Kirkby, Charles Parsons, Nigel Pritchard, Hillary Wood, Caryll Ziegler.

About the Speechworks

The Speechworks specializes in one-to-one presentation skills training for public figures, sports personalities, and people in business.

Every member of The Speechworks team is a professional actor, director or writer with many years experience of working in film, TV and theatre. They teach the skills and techniques that are the performers' tools of the trade and show clients how to use them with confidence.

www.thespeechworks.co.uk

'Good Communication is vital in all areas of life. Whether you are on the world stage or engaging with business colleagues or friends, Teach Yourself The Clinton Factor takes the best from a master of communication and delivers effective strategies for us mere mortals!'

Lesley Upham, Director of Communications Thatcham

'In my opinion Bill Clinton is one of a small band of truly great communicators. Teach Yourself The Clinton Factor pays specific attention to the structure and emotional aspects of his approach – this learning technique has allowed me to communicate much more effectively.'

James Henderson, Operations Director William Hill PLC

'A knowledge and total understanding of what you are talking about is essential. Believe in what you are saying and PLEASE make your delivery interesting and engaging – keep it short, cut out all the jargon, speak in normal everyday language and you will have them hanging on your every word!'

Bill Dod, TV Presenter – Anchor Russia Today

'The art of effective communication is looking, listening, thinking and choosing the right language to create the desired effect – this book does exactly that!'

Major General Andy Salmon OBE, Royal Marines – Commander UK Amphibious Forces

'Just by observing a charismatic communicator like Bill Clinton, we can all learn much about how to connect with people in what we say and how we say it.'

Donna Johnson, Head of Organizational Development EMI

'No. One does not have to be an admirer of Clinton the man to recognize Clinton as a supreme communicator, if not the supreme communicator of his times.

Why? Because behind a surgically precise use of language there is a fallible human being who recognizes the fallibilities of his hearers. It is a potent cocktail.'

Roger Bramble, Former High Sheriff of Greater London

'Great communication is about performing brilliantly well. Everyone in public life can and should learn from Clinton. He has to be one of the finest communicators the US has ever produced.'

Ray Burdis, actor, producer, and director

'Bill Clinton is the consummate professional in terms of presentation prowess, he seems to know exactly how to address an audience, time after time after time.'

Councillor Robert Davis DL, Chief Whip Westminster City Council and Chairman of The London Mayors' Association

'The difference in communication is between people who speak a lot but say nothing and those whose meaning is grasped crisply, poignantly and whose message is brilliantly effective – Bill Clinton definitely falls into the second category.'

Bruce Priday, Chairman FT Consultants

'Communicating effectively, powerfully and persuasively as Clinton does is a skill all senior business professionals would do well to master, or at least attempt to master.'

Nick Ivey, Senior Partner Bates Wells & Braithwaite – lawyers

'Bill Clinton intuitively knows that delivering a speech is an emotional experience akin to having a baby. He will have carefully nurtured the story before allowing it to burst upon his audience at the moment every one of them recognizes their part in it's conception. Everybody in the audience then knows, from that moment, their life will never be the same because of what they heard that was said just for them!'

Garvis Snook, CEO Rok   (Voted CEO of year 2007)

'This book is not your stereotypical text on how to present. More importantly it focuses upon the skills and psychology of good communication, and understanding our audiences' perceptions of us as people.'

Dr V. Hill, Chartered Consultant Clinical Psychologist BSC, MSC, PSYCH D

Author photo © Brian Rasic/Rex Features

01

introduction

So what is The Clinton Factor?

'Big things are expected of us, and nothing big ever came of being small.'

Clinton's Inaugural Address, 20 January 1997

This is not a political book or a biography. It is neither a pro nor anti-Clinton book. This is a book about William Jefferson Clinton's great communication skills. Whatever our political standpoint very few people could fail to acknowledge that Bill Clinton is one of the world's greatest communicators. He's certainly one of the finest public speakers of our time. He's good on camera and he does great TV interviews but what is it that makes him so accomplished at what he does? What is it that gives him the ability to connect with people so effortlessly? What is it that gives him the power to present, both himself and what he says in such an engaging, effective and memorable way. And how does he do it (or seem to do it) with such effortless ease?

Well let's first look at the man and the impression he makes on us. He's tall and reasonably good-looking. He has a pleasant voice, charisma and charm. He was also once the most powerful person in the world. That's not a bad start when it comes to being a good communicator. But it's more than those things. It's much more. What Bill Clinton has, and what makes him such a consummate communicator, is The Clinton Factor.

Teach Yourself The Clinton Factor will reveal to you the secrets of the master communicator and the techniques he uses. The Clinton Factor is made up of three essential pillars that are the central components of good communication skills: Story, Status and Focus. By exploring the world of story, status and focus, or SSF, we don't just gain an understanding of Clinton's ability, we also begin to see how we can all improve our communication and presentation skills.

Most people fear public speaking more than death

As Jerry Seinfeld once observed, surveys tell us that most people fear public speaking more than death! So, as Jerry said, if you're at a funeral you're better off in the coffin than giving the eulogy. That's easy to believe it isn't it? How many of us today, in our business lives, have to make presentations or speeches? Almost all of us. And how many of us are totally relaxed at the prospect and completely confident in our ability to perform brilliantly? Not many of us, that's for sure. But Bill always seems to be relaxed. Bill is always confident. Bill always gets his message across.

One of the biggest reasons most people don't relish the thought of standing up in public and speaking, or making an important presentation at work, is that it makes us feel nervous. Anxiety, nerves, butterflies in the stomach – whatever you call them, they are all completely normal. Professional actors, who've studied technique for many years and continue to train throughout their careers, still get nerves before they go on stage or perform in front of camera. Indeed, many actors would say, that it's being a little nervous that heightens their performance.

An important part of the art of public speaking is dealing with our anxieties and one of the best ways of doing that is to focus on the needs of our audience rather than on our own. Anyone who has to stand and deliver has an obligation to put their audience at ease and in a comfortable position to receive the message. The last thing an audience wants is to be on the edge of their seats worrying about the person speaking.

We certainly do not have any worries or concerns when watching Bill Clinton. He seems to have a deep understanding of the fact that the most important part of the audience–speaker relationship is the audience. Bill Clinton displays complete control over audience comfort through his mastery of the three primary elements of good speaker–audience relations – story, status and focus. And because of his understanding of SSF he's always prepared, with no apparent signs of nervousness.

Story

> *'There have been great societies that did not use the wheel, but there have been no societies that did not tell stories.'*
>
> Ursula K. Le Guin

Whatever the message we are trying to communicate to our audience, getting the story right is absolutely crucial. Storytelling is our fundamental mode of communication. As humans, we've been telling stories since time immemorial. We start telling stories from the moment we learn to speak. We tell stories because this is the best way of getting people to understand information. But because telling stories is what makes our messages accessible and memorable, it is crucial that we get the story right. The most brilliant delivery in the world will not save badly constructed material. Paying great attention to the construction of our stories, creating a fluid journey for our audience and bringing the story to life are all essential aspects of good storytelling.

It really doesn't matter what the situation – once we have stood up to speak we have entered the world of show business. With that goes a duty to entertain and engage. So it is very important, therefore, to have a *good* story. Many people in the business world may think, 'I have to convey serious pieces of information when I give presentations – there's no room for fooling around telling stories!' But they're wrong. As part of our role with The Speechworks, we coach and train many senior directors of large corporate organizations in acting and writing skills. More often than not these directors are very quick to tell us how dull and dry their material is and how the content of their presentations could never be engaging or exciting. We are equally as quick to tell them that this is just their perception. Often their assumption that the message is not interesting is the root of the problem with a presentation or speech. Whatever the material, there is always a story – with a beginning, a middle and an end – waiting to get out. Most of our daily communications have the 'beginnings, middles and ends' that all good stories consist of. So making sure that our speeches, presentations and more formal addresses have the same story structure is vital.

When we listen to Bill Clinton speak there can be no doubt that he has given special attention to assembling his speech and telling his story. His stories are alive with enthusiasm and spontaneity. He picks us up, takes us on a journey and deposits us exactly where he wants us to be. *Teach Yourself The Clinton Factor* will give you some essential rules, models and tips on how you can get the story right.

Status

> 'At a round table there is no dispute about place.'

> Italian proverb

Bill Clinton's delivery always gives us a sense that he is sharing something of himself with us. We feel at ease with him and personally addressed by him. We find him warm and approachable. He seems accessible and strong. This is because he adopts the right level of status.

If you look up 'status' in the dictionary it will say: 'Status: Latin, standing, posture'. This may indicate that it is something physical. Yes, it is physical but it is also mental, vocal and emotional. Status is how we perceive people and how people perceive us. Status can, of course, be determined by hierarchy and positions of seniority but that's not what status is really all about. Status is about how we perceive people no matter what their position. It enables us to make decisions about how to react to people. When we meet someone for the first time we subconsciously ask ourselves three questions.

1 What sex is that person?
2 How old are they?
3 What is their status?

Actors study status when training and rehearsing. It is important that actors understand the extremes of status to portray the character they are playing effectively. People in business or public life do not have the luxury of experimenting with status in the way that actors do. They have to get it right first time.

The status scale of 1 to 10

Finding the right level of status to be effective in our business, public or personal lives is the central pillar of The Clinton Factor. On a status scale of 1 to 10 we need to be hitting the middle status ground of 5 to 7 every time. We don't want to appear aloof or arrogant (10) nor do we want to timidly apologize for ourselves (1).

Bill Clinton gets his status level right every time – when making a speech, when being interviewed, even when out in public. After the horrors of 9/11 when Bush looked like a rabbit caught in the headlights, Clinton was walking the streets hugging people. The public were literally throwing themselves into his arms! Why? Because he was open, warm, receptive and strong. Which was exactly what the American people needed at that time.

It is very difficult to argue with, or take offence at, the middle ground – an open and neutral status. It is the closest we are ever likely to get to being and acting the same with everyone we meet. When we first started working with business clients on status we asked a clinical psychologist, if it was possible for someone to be the same with everyone. The psychologist thought for a moment and replied, 'Yes, but they would probably have to be sectioned.' So the next time you hear someone say, 'Oh, I'm the same with everyone – king, queen, peasant, pauper – what you see is what you get with me,' run a mile because they are clearly raving mad!

The right level

Getting the level of status right isn't just applicable to those who have to stand and speak. It is just as important in every other area of our working lives. When coaching a senior director of a FTSE 100 company recently, we soon discovered that it wasn't just his presentation style that the training department wanted us to look at. They also wanted us to change his behaviour in the workplace. This particular individual was tall and physically quite imposing. He also, rather proudly, assumed a very high level of status vocally, mentally and emotionally. He almost seemed to enjoy stomping around like Godzilla and bawling at people.

This was a challenging brief but we came up with a strategy that satisfied both agendas. He was very eager to learn about The Clinton Factor and how it could improve his presentation skills. So our plan was to work heavily on status. In order to seamlessly adopt the open, warm, receptive level of status required to be an effective presenter we insisted that this level be maintained at all times. We asked him to check his level of status with every piece of communication he had in his working day. The result was a behavioural transformation with his colleagues. He found that hitting the right level of status changed how he behaved and also improved how he was perceived by others.

By hitting that 5 to 7 level of status Bill Clinton makes himself totally accessible to his audiences. Anything lower would result in a reduction of audience respect and so close him off. Anything higher would run the risk of making an audience feel that they were being spoken down to. The chapters in this book on status will give a great insight into the value and importance of achieving that Clinton level of status.

Focus

'Act the part and you will become the part.'

William James

The third element of The Clinton Factor is focus, the icing on the cake. Bill Clinton has focus in spades. And whether he knows it or not, he has a Russian theatre director and acting innovator, born in 1863, to thank for it.

Konstantin Sergeyevich Stanislavski was the co-founder of the Moscow Art Theatre, the founder of the first acting system, (Stanislavski's System) and a great exponent of the naturalist school of thought. He was also the inspiration behind Lee Strasbourg's 'Method' School of Acting in New York City to which many acting greats subscribe including Robert De Niro, Dustin Hoffman, Judi Dench, Kate Winslett and Anthony Hopkins to name just a few. See pages 134–36 for more on Stanislavski.

Stanislavski's circles of concentration

Stanislavski's circles of concentration or attention are the professional actor's fundamental source of on-stage focus. They are an unbelievably powerful tool that should not be restricted solely to the world of film and theatre. Stanislavski once said: 'If the ability to receive the creative mood in its full measure is given to genius by nature, then perhaps ordinary people may reach a like state after a great deal of hard work with themselves – not in its full measure, but at least in part.'

Whether or not Bill Clinton has acquired his creative focus naturally, it is without doubt one of the most powerful weapons in his armoury. As we know, when he speaks we get a real sense that he is sharing something of himself with us. This is partially due to the level of status he adopts, but also because of his extraordinary ability to manage the focus of his performance and the focus of his audience. Some would say that Bill Clinton has a certain '*Je ne sais quoi*', others might say that it's 'star quality', but we know that it is in fact focus.

The ability to use and harness the three circles of concentration turns a competent address into a truly compelling performance. Would an audience prefer to sit through an adequately delivered address or be highly entertained? Great performances have a huge impact on us, which is why much emphasis must be placed on the subject of focus and concentration. Take two very different performers in two different situations with two very different subject matters. Martin Luther King with his 'I have a Dream' speech delivered in Washington DC in 1963, and Robert De Niro playing the lonely, deranged Vietnam war veteran in *Taxi Driver*. Both expertly manage our focus with the crafted distribution of their own focus and technique. Bill Clinton does exactly the same when he speaks to an audience, an interviewer, whoever.

Shakespeare said, 'All the world's a stage,' and he wasn't wrong. As coaches in the skills of presentation we have gained enormous pleasure from introducing the world of commerce and public life to the theories and practices of theatre and screen. There is an increasing commonality between people in business, public figures, politicians and entertainers. Today, more than ever, it's all about performance. And performance is all about focus. *Teach Yourself The Clinton Factor* explains Stanislavski' s circles of concentration and how you can learn and apply them with maximum effect.

Who can benefit from the The Clinton Factor?

Achieving a good level of The Clinton Factor with story, status and focus is not rocket science but it does require some degree of application. It doesn't matter what kind of address we have to make – a wedding speech, a business presentation, a conference address – the three basic components of SFF are common to all that we deliver. If we know our subject well and get the broad strokes right the detail will take care of itself. The Clinton Factor forms a solid three-point platform to inspire confidence in all types of address. You'll find that having a simple technical base to underpin your delivery technique can be very empowering and highly effective.

What you'll learn from The Clinton Factor

- How any presentation or speech can and should be turned into a story.
- How by adopting the right level of status, like Bill Clinton, we can project ourselves as being open, warm, receptive and strong.
- How learning to focus, like Bill Clinton, can transform a presentation or speech into a compelling performance.

Sections of 'to dos' and exercises

At various points in this book you'll find brief sections of 'to dos' and exercises. These will give you the opportunity to explore in more depth different aspects of The Clinton Factor. If you'd like to develop some of The Clinton Factor for yourself you should give these activities a try.

> *'We should, all of us, be filled with gratitude and humility for our present progress and prosperity. We should be filled with awe and joy at what lies over the horizon. And we should be filled with absolute determination to make the most of it.'*
>
> Bill Clinton

part one

introducing Bill Clinton

02

about William Jefferson Clinton

Humble beginnings

Bill Clinton was born William Jefferson Blythe III on 19 August 1946, in Hope, a small town in Arkansas. He never knew his father, William Jefferson Blythe Jr, a travelling salesman, because he was tragically killed in a car accident three months before his son's birth.

His mother, Virginia, married car dealer Roger Clinton, of Hot Springs, Arkansas when Bill was four. Bill adopted the family name Clinton later while at high school.

Education

At high school in Hot Springs, Clinton excelled as a student in most subjects and was a student leader and talented saxophonist. He enjoyed English, with his English teacher making Shakespeare's *Julius Caesar* come alive by giving it a contemporary twist: he and his classmates put the meaning of the play into ordinary words.

Clinton thought about a career in medicine and music but it is reputed that his attention turned to politics after meeting President John F Kennedy in the White House Rose Garden on a Boy's Nation school trip to Washington DC. In his senior year at high school, Clinton was devastated by the news when his teacher told him that President Kennedy had been shot and probably killed.

Bill Clinton graduated from Georgetown University School of Foreign Services in 1968 and spent the summer of '67 working as an intern for Arkansas Senator Fulbright.

After graduation he won a Rhodes scholarship to Oxford University where he studied Government from 1968 to 1970. On returning to the United States Clinton studied law at Yale and gained a law degree in 1973. After graduation, he returned to Arkansas where he worked as a law professor. In 1974 Clinton ran for the House of Representatives but was defeated. Two years later, in 1976, he was elected Attorney General of Arkansas without opposition.

In 1975, Bill Clinton married Hillary Rodham (see the appendices for her biography). They had met while law students together at Yale. In 1980 their daughter and only child, Chelsea Victoria Clinton, was born.

Governor of Arkansas

Bill was elected governor of Arkansas in 1978 at the age of 32 and was the youngest governor in the country. He failed to be re-elected in the general election of 1980 but regained the governorship two years later and served until 1993. During his 12 years in office, Governor Clinton earned national recognition for his progressive programmes, particularly the attempt to improve the state's economy and public education system.

42nd President of the United States

In 1987 the media speculated that Clinton, then known as the Boy Governor because of his age and youthful appearance, might enter the race for the Democratic nominations in1988. But Clinton waited until 1992 when he secured the Democratic Party nomination and went on to defeat Republican President George Bush, and independent candidate Ross Perot in the 1992 presidential race. The election of Clinton brought to an end an era of Republican rule of the White House that went back 12 years. His election also meant that Democrats controlled both branches of Congress, the House of Representatives and the Senate, for the first time since the late 1970s.

William Clinton was inaugurated on 20 January 1993 as the 42nd President of the United States. In his inaugural address he famously said: 'There is nothing wrong with America that cannot be cured by what is right with America.'

In 1996, Clinton was re-elected President defeating Republican Bob Dole and Reform candidate Ross Perot. With this victory he became the first Democrat to be re-elected for a second term since Franklin D Roosevelt in the 1930s.

During his time as President, the country enjoyed the lowest unemployment rate in modern times, the lowest inflation in 30 years and the highest home ownership in the country's history. He proposed the first balanced budget in decades and achieved a budget surplus.

Lewinsky and impeachment

In his second term, character issues began to re-emerge and Clinton came under increasing pressure from independent counsel, Kenneth Starr. In January 1998, Clinton was called to testify in a sexual harassment suit brought against him by a former Arkansas state employee. During the hearing Clinton denied that he had had a sexual relationship with a young White House intern, Monica Lewinsky, and that he had attempted to cover it up. A federal judge threw out the sexual harassment suit in April 1998 but the Lewinsky affair had caught the interest of the world's media.

On 17 August 1998, Clinton became the first US president to testify in front of a grand jury in an investigation into his possible criminal conduct. He addressed the nation on TV that evening and admitted to having had an 'inappropriate relationship' with Lewinsky.

Despite all this, Clinton's popularity seemed to remain high among the American people. Poll after poll showed the American population's general disapproval of a trial, but Congress moved forward with impeachment proceedings.

On 19 December, Clinton became only the second president in American history to be impeached. Two of the four articles of impeachment were passed, and votes were drawn along party lines. A trial in the Senate in January and February 1999 found the President not guilty of the charges brought against him and he was acquitted on both counts.

President Clinton apologized for his conduct and vowed to keep working as hard as he could for the American people. Bill Clinton remained popular with the public throughout his two terms as President. He left office with the highest end-of-term approval rating of any President since Dwight D Eisenhower.

After Office

Since leaving Office Clinton has embarked on a highly successful career as public speaker, travelling the world speaking to huge audiences on a range of issues. He is also involved in humanitarian work and has created the William J Clinton Foundation, which promotes and addresses international cause like global warming, HIV/AIDS and third world poverty.

His personal biography *My Life* was published in 2004 and sold more than 400,000 copies in the United States on in its first day of release, the highest ever sales for a non-fiction book. It also topped the Amazon.com non-fiction bestseller list in the United States, England, France and Japan.

Clinton is also a double Grammy winner. In 2004, he won a golden gramophone statuette in the best spoken word album for children category. The next year, he won another Grammy in the best-spoken word album category for the recording of his best-selling autobiography *My Life*.

> '*Words are, of course, the most powerful drug used by mankind.*'
>
> Rudyard Kipling

> '*If I am to speak ten minutes, I need a week for preparation; if fifteen minutes, three days; if half an hour, two days; if an hour, I am ready now.*'
>
> Woodrow Wilson

part two

story

two

In this part you will learn:
- how to construct and edit a fluid and entertaining message
- how to create your story with performance in mind
- how your story can impact on your listeners.

03

what is a story?

One of the reasons Clinton is such a powerful and effective communicator is because he understands the importance of story. But what exactly do we mean by story?

Definitions

There are many dictionary definitions of story. But let's look at this one below.

> '*A piece of narrative, tale of any length, told or printed in prose or verse, based on either true or fictitious events, legend, myth, anecdote, and designed to interest, amuse or instruct the hearer or reader.*'

So a story or narrative, which incidentally comes from the Latin, *narrare*, which means 'to recount', can be:

- a tale of any length,
- told or printed,
- true or fictitious,
- designed to interest, amuse or instruct.

Look at the basic framework of a story:

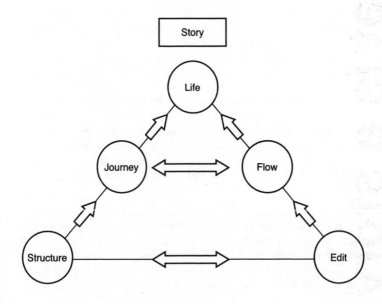

Why do we tell stories?

As humans we have been telling stories since we first developed the power of speech. It's our most natural form of communication and has been with us since our beginning. Indeed some people maintain that it is storytelling that defines us as human beings.

Imagine our ancestors way back in the dawn of time returning from a hunt. They would have stories to tell of how big the mammoth was that somehow got away. They would have stories of how they were almost killed by a fierce and terrible sabre-toothed tiger. They would have stories of bravery, success and happiness. They would tell tales of disappointment, fear and death. Stories with a happy ending or stories with an unhappy ending. We are still telling those basic stories today.

It is interesting when looking back to the stories and communication skills of primitive man to think that maybe the cave paintings of animals were actually drawn to help illustrate the stories that were being told. The earliest known example of a PowerPoint® presentation perhaps?

Passing on information and knowledge

The oral tradition of storytelling also had a very important function. It allowed us to pass on information and knowledge from group to group and from generation to generation. In ages gone, stories were used to explain the many events that were beyond the control of man – droughts, floods, storms and thunder. These works of nature must have been both awe inspiring and frightening to our ancestors. Stories helped them to come to terms with these events and also prepared the next generation to be aware of them. Stories about gods, goddesses, heroes and heroines helped people develop and protect a shared belief system, which would bind them closer together. While stories with a moral element were ways of helping the development of customs and behavioural codes for the benefit of all.

Almost every culture in the world has a tradition of storytelling. It is also interesting to note that the storytellers were often the elders of the community. They told their stories to pass on valuable information and wisdom, ensuring that it would not be lost. Elder storytellers were always highly respected members of their society. Those who could tell a great tale of heroic deeds or amazing escape from disaster were very highly regarded and valued by their people.

Clinton knows that story is just as powerful and effective a force now as it always has been. Indeed, today, it is probably more powerful than ever.

Stories in the media and web age

In the media age, story as a form of communication is probably more pervasive now than at any time in history. We are surrounded by stories: news stories on TV, in the press and on the internet; soap opera stories, stories in film, theatre and books; gossip stories about celebrities that start on the street and are spread around the world via the web. Stories are universal – another reason why we respond to storytelling so much.

The oldest surviving story

Story is truly an ancient form of communication. The oldest surviving story is the epic poem Gilgamesh, which tells the tale of a mythological Sumerian king who is part human and part god. It dates back to Ancient Mesopotamia around 2000 BC.

Key points

- Stories are our most natural form of communication.
- The development of stories allowed information, knowledge and wisdom to be passed from group to group and from generation to generation.
- Almost every culture in the world has a tradition of storytelling.
- Telling a story has always been associated with highly respected members of society.

To do: Now you tell a story

To help you absorb the information on story from this section, here's a simple exercise to try.

Imagine that you are prehistoric caveman or cavewoman. You've just returned to your cave after a hard day's hunting. Your partner is waiting for you by the fire. Tell a story about your day's hunt. Write out your story, keeping it between 50 and 100 words if you can. It is important that you find the time to do this exercise, as we will refer back to your story later.

'When people talk, listen completely. Most people never listen.'

Ernest Hemingway

04

getting the story right

Types of story

There are many types and genre of story. Here are just a few of them:

- fable
- parable
- myth
- fairy tale
- legend

Fable

The fable is one of the most enduring forms of story. It is generally brief and features animals, plants, forces of nature or inanimate objects that are given human characteristics or qualities. They illustrate a moral lesson known as the moral of the story.

Interestingly the word fable is derived from the Latin word *fabula* which means 'story'. Some of the best-known fables are Aesop's fables, said to have been written by the Greek slave Aesop in the sixth century.

Someone who writes fables is known as a fabulist while the word fabulous literally means 'about a fable or fables'. We will look at fables in more detail later in the book. In the meantime you will find Aesop's *The Hare and the Tortoise* at the end of this section.

Parable

A parable is brief story like a fable except that it uses humans instead of animals, plants, forces of nature or inanimate objects to tell the tale. A parable illustrates a moral or religious lesson. The parables of Jesus such as *The Prodigal Son*, *The Lost Sheep*, *The Talents* and *The Good Samaritan* are probably the best known, but at the end of this chapter you will find the traditional Jewish parable of *The Rooster Prince*.

Myth

A myth is a traditional story usually involving supernatural or fantastical individuals or gods. Ancient people often used myths to explain aspects of nature and the world they lived in that they could not fully understand.

Fairy tale

Fairy tales are essentially fables in a magical setting often based on a series of highly improbable events. They always happen 'once upon a time...'.

Legend

A legend is a traditional story often about human actions that are thought to have some historical basis. *The Holy Grail*, *William Tell* and *King Arthur and the Knights of the Round Table* are all examples of legends.

Telling a great story

So what has any of this got to do with Bill Clinton's ability to tell a great story? Well, when we look at say the parable of *The Rooster Prince*, the legend of *King Arthur and the Knights of the Round Table* and Aesop's *The Hare and the Tortoise*, what do they have in common?

Nothing! You're probably thinking, these stories have nothing in common whatsoever. But they do. And what they have in common is absolutely central to the power of story. It's central to the power of Bill Clinton as a communicator and it's central to this book.

The one thing all these forms of story have in common is structure. By structure we mean the way the story is shaped with a beginning, a middle and an end.

Look at the two stories below, *The Hare and the Tortoise* and *The Rooster Prince*. They are two very different stories, from different cultures and from different periods. But they share the same structure: beginning, middle and end.

The Hare and the Tortoise: An Aesop fable retold

Once in Made-up-animal-land there was a very rapid and speedy hare. He often boasted to the other animals about how super-fast he could run.

One day, a tortoise heard hare boasting yet again about his amazing speed and running ability. Bored and irritated by the hare's constant bragging, the tortoise decided to challenge him to a race. All of the other animals were utterly amazed that the slow and steady tortoise should want to race the hare.

When race day came, all the animals of Made-up-animal-land gathered to watch the contest. The hare and the tortoise took their positions at the starting line.

On your marks, get set, go! The race began.

The hare darted off and was almost out of sight at once. He ran for a while longer and then, totally confident of victory, he stopped for a rest. Hare stretched out under a tree and fell asleep, thinking that the race was as good as won.

The tortoise slowly plodded on and on at his usual leisurely pace. As the tortoise approached the finishing line the animals started cheering loudly. This woke the hare who jumped up and began running again. But he was too late, the tortoise had crossed the finishing line. Slow and steady had won the race.

The Rooster Prince: A tradtional Jewish parable

Once there was a prince who went insane and started believing that he was a rooster. He took off his clothes and sat naked under the table, clucking and pecking at the food, and eating it off the floor.

Naturally, the King and Queen were absolutely horrified to see the prince, the heir to the throne of the kingdom, behave like this. They asked all sorts of doctors, sages and wise men to treat him and cure him but nothing seemed to work. The King and Queen were in despair.

Then one day a new wise man arrived at the castle and said that he could cure the Prince. The King and Queen were desperate and so decided to give the new wise man a chance.

The wise man took off his clothes and sat naked under the table with the prince, telling him that he was a rooster as well. The King and Queen were of course shocked. But by sitting under the table and telling him that he was rooster too, the wise man gradually got to know the Prince.

After a while the wise man told the prince that a rooster *can* wear clothes. So the prince put on his clothes. The wise man then told the prince that a rooster can sit at a table. So the prince started sitting at the table

The wise man then told the prince that a rooster *can* eat food off a plate with a knife and fork. So the Prince started eating off a plate with a knife and fork.

Soon the Prince was acting like a human again and was pronounced completely cured.

Key points

- There are many types and genre of story (e.g. folk tale, tall tale, bedtime story, love story, ghost story, horror story and urban legend).
- All sorts of stories, from all sorts of cultures share the same structure.
- All stories should have a beginning, a middle and an end. This may seem obvious but it is often forgotten when people are constructing stories.

To do: Tell a story with a beginning, a middle and an end

Read the *The Rooster Prince* and *The Hare and the Tortoise*. Can you see the beginning, middle and end structure? Where does the middle start and end?

Now look back at the hunter story you wrote for the previous chapter. Does it have a beginning, a middle and an end. If it does, great. If it doesn't, rewrite the story making sure that it has a solid beginning, middle and end structure.

'The more elaborate our means of communication, the less we communicate.'

Joseph Priestly

05

the importance of good structure

The importance of structure in a story cannot be emphasized too much. Just as we recognize and admire the structure of a beautiful building that has been conceived and designed by a talented architect, so as humans we recognize and admire the structure of a well-crafted story.

We may do this sub-consciously but the structure of a story impacts on us greatly. Think of people leaving the cinema having seen a movie which told a great story that really resonated with them. They are inspired and touched by what they've seen.

Now think of a film you've seen that you didn't enjoy. Chances are that in that film it was the structure that didn't work – it was the story that didn't satisfy. You left the cinema feeling cheated and let down. The emotional response you were hoping for and expecting just didn't happen.

The three-act play

Most stage plays have three acts. Most great movies can be seen as three-act stories. Three seems to be a magic number when imparting information. So when we're delivering a message, making a speech or presentation it's clearly a good idea to keep to this three-act form.

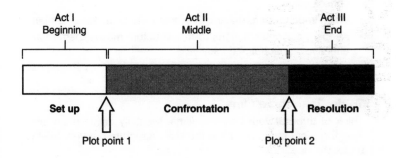

three-act structure

If you look at the diagram above, you'll see that in the three-act structure we have three other factors:

1 the set up
2 the confrontation
3 the resolution.

Now in a Hollywood movie this could be:

1 A cop finds his best friend brutally murdered and vows to find the killer.
2 He sets off on his quest to avenge his friend's death.
3 He finds the killer and brings him to justice.

But how would this relate to a business presentation or speech? How does it fit in with The Clinton Factor? If you look at any of Clinton's speeches reproduced in this book you'll see that they all have those three elements. There is the set up or introduction, the confrontation or issues that need to be addressed/problems that need to be resolved, and finally the resolution or conclusion.

So next time you are asked to make a business presentation think of it as a short movie. Make sure it has a shape that your audience will find familiar. If you do this then your audience are more likely to respond to your presentation in the way you intended.

Key points

- Most great movies and stage plays have a three-act structure.
- As humans we respond to this structure sometimes sub-consciously.
- When imparting information, three seems to be a magic number.
- Keeping our presentations to this structure makes them more effective, impactful and satisfying.

To do: Take three films

Think of three of your favourite films. Mentally divide them into their three-act structure. Write the story structure out very briefly under the headings.

- set up
- confrontation
- resolution

'Many attempts to communicate are nullified by saying too much.'

Robert Greenleaf

06 does the story work?

Information comes alive when we impart it to people as a story. We have now also seen that a story has very simple structure and form. So it really shouldn't be difficult to create a story based on some simple facts that we have to impart.

Let's imagine we're going to prepare a presentation or speech to give to a group of business colleagues. We know what information we have to impart but we first have to decide how to tell it in a story. And we have to make sure it's a story that will interest our audience. After all, if our audience are not interested they won't remember very much.

Here is a very simple and brief story:

> *Once a man was feeling a bit hungry. He went to a shop, got some food and ate it. He wasn't hungry anymore. The end.*

Now that story follows the rules we've outlined so far. It's short and to the point. It has a beginning, middle and end – the three-act structure. So what's wrong with it? It's boring, deadly dull, about as exciting as watching paint dry! So as well as the right structure a story needs to have the right content. It needs to have some impact.

Let's look at our boring story about a man eating again and see if we can make it more interesting:

> *A man was starving. He hadn't eaten for days and days. So in desperation he broke into an exclusive and very expensive delicatessen and stole some food. He ate and ate until he was completely full. It was the most delicious food he'd ever tasted. It was like nectar. The end.*

As you can see, it doesn't take much to make even the most boring tale seem more interesting.

- The beginning has been changed to make it more compelling – there's something at stake now.
- The middle has been made more dramatic – there's more at stake here too, the man is breaking the law.
- The end or resolution has been made more satisfying. The food the man ate tasted like nectar.

We should bear this example in mind in our business presentations. Bill Clinton always makes sure that the content he delivers has impact. And that it's all based on telling people a story. Nothing illustrates this story and content relationship as well as this extract below from the prologue of his autobiography.

In Bill's autobiography he tells a story about when, as a young man just out of law school, he wrote a list of things he wanted to achieve in his life. Under the A list he wrote:

> '... to be a good man, have a good marriage and children, have good friends, make a successful political life and write a great book.'

The prologue ends with this:

> 'My life in politics was a joy. I loved campaigns and I loved governing. I always tried to keep things moving in the right directions, to give more people a chance to live their dreams, to lift people's spirits and to bring them together. That's the way I kept score. As for the great book, who knows? It sure is a good story.'

Key point

- As well as the right structure a story needs to have the right content – it needs impact!

To do: Giving it a bit more impact

Look back again at your rewritten (or original) hunter story. Can you give it a bit more impact? Aim to grab and keep your reader's attention.

> 'The problem with communication... is the illusion that it has been accomplished.'
>
> George Bernard Shaw

> 'Stories are the most important thing in the world. Without stories, we wouldn't be human at all.'
>
> Philip Pullman

07

edit, edit and edit again

Sometimes we all have difficulty in being concise in our communications, but when preparing a speech or a presentation it's vital to be as concise and succinct as possible. Clinton shows that time and time again. When you are concise in what you say, clarity often follows.

So you've worked out your content, you know your story, you know the main messages you want your audience to take away. So all you need to do is sit down and write out your presentation or speech.

If you study Clinton and other great speakers you'll know that they also have the edge here. What they do is edit, cut, streamline and trim the speech down to a level where it's as succinct, clear and memorable as possible.

Discipline and ruthlessness

This isn't easy. As Mark Twain said: 'I didn't have time to write a short letter, so I wrote a long one instead.' It takes discipline and ruthlessness to edit, edit, edit, but every time you do, the end result is a better, more impactful speech. A good rule of thumb that some professionals use is to attempt to cut your first draft by between a third and a half. As soon as you've finished your first draft, start cutting and keep cutting. And don't forget that to tell an audience something doesn't mean that you have to tell them everything. Work on the principle of sorting out the 'need to know' from the 'nice to know', and discard the latter. Cut out information that your audience won't miss if they are not told it. If in doubt leave it out, is a great maxim to help you in this process.

Less is more

This phrase 'less is more' is often associated with the architect and furniture designer Ludwig Mies van der Rohe. As one of the pioneering founders of modern architecture he believed in simplicity of style. (He also incidentally designed the Martin Luther King Jr Memorial Library in Washington DC.)

If 'less is more' gives simplicity and style to buildings and architecture then it's even more applicable to presenting and the spoken word. To Clinton the idea of 'less is more' seems to come naturally.

Key points

- Always edit and edit, again and again.
- When we are concise clarity follows.
- Less really is more.
- Keeping our presentations to this structure makes them more effective, impactful and satisfying.

To do: Edit, cut, trim

Read the two stories – *The Hare and the Tortosie* and *The Rooster Prince* – again. Do a word count of both. Now rewrite both the stories shortening them by a third. Observe what you decide to cut and why.

Now repeat the process with original versions of *The Hare and the Tortoise* and *The Rooster Prince*. But be as ruthless as possible with your edit. Cut the length down this time to a half. Edit, edit, edit.

'Be sincere; be brief; be seated.'

Franklin D. Roosevelt

08

bring it to life

So now, like Clinton, you should have the following aspects of your speech or presentation all fixed in your mind:

1 The structure
2 The story you are going to tell
3 The content, edited and streamlined.

You should also know what the objectives of your speech are.

• What do you want to achieve?
• What do you want your audience to think or believe?
• How do you want them to feel when you finish your speech?

All that remains for you to do now is to bring your speech or presentation to life. You are about to use your story to take your audience on a journey. You are going to pick them up and carry them with you – all with just the power of speech – and deposit them somewhere else.

'How am I going to do that?' you may be wondering. But Clinton does exactly that time after time. And if he can learn to do it, so can you.

We will discuss some ways of bringing your presentation to life through performance in the status and focus parts of the book. But there are many techniques you can learn from story.

The power of story – the range of your voice

Part of the power of story is that we are told stories from a very early age. As children we loved stories of princes and princesses, of magical lands. We were scared by stories of wicked witches. We were enchanted by stories of mythical beasts.

We also love telling children stories ourselves. And when we tell children stories do we always tell them in the same monotonous flat voice? No, of course we don't. We bring them to life with the range of our voice. We use different voices for the goody and the baddy. We cackle like witches or wizards for dramatic effect. We in effect become performers. And that is what we should do when we present to any audience. (We mean become performers not cackle like witches or wizards obviously!)

Jokes and shaggy dog stories

When people tell jokes and humorous stories to friends they do exactly the same thing. They use their voice to bring their story to life. They use their hands, arms, facial expressions and body language to emphasize a particular aspect of the story. They become performers – quite naturally and without any hint of embarrassment or awkwardness. So one easy way for us to bring the speech or presentation to life is to begin to think like a performer.

Your choice of words

Part of The Clinton Factor and the appeal of the man as a presenter is his control of the words he uses. His use of language is quite often simply masterly. He gives us the impression that each and every word has been carefully chosen for a reason. We too should copy Bill and make sure that the words we use sound precise, measured and carefully selected.

Here are four ways of saying essentially the same thing:

1 I tell you today...
2 I am here to inform you...
3 I've got something to say...
4 Listen to this...

You'll notice that although they say the same thing they have totally different meanings and nuances.

Key points

- Use your story to take your audience on a journey.
- Use the range of your voice to help bring your story to life.
- Choose your words carefully and they will work harder for you.
- Think like a performer.

To do: Bring it to life

Tell *The Rooster Prince* story to a colleague, a friend or your partner. Use your voice to mimic the characters. Use your body to emphasize parts of the story. Entertain them for a few minutes. They'll enjoy it – it's a great story after all.

09

rhetoric and oratory today

We can learn other techniques to bring our story to life from rhetoric, oratory and simple writing skills.

Rhetoric – the art, skill, technique or study of using language effectively and persuasively – was first mentioned in Homer's *Iliad*. But much of it is as powerful now as it is ever was. Oratory is quite simply the skill of public speaking.

Clinton and other great communicators have a deep understanding of these techniques. They sometimes seem to use them almost instinctively. But we can all, with a little training, start using them intelligently and appropriately.

Alliteration

This is the repetition of the same sound at the beginning of several words in a sequence. It is useful for stressing an important point or for making something more memorable.

> **Examples**
>
> *'Veni, vidi, vici.'*
>
> Julius Caesar
>
> *'Let us go forth to lead the land we love.'*
>
> J. F. Kennedy
>
> *'And our nation itself is testimony to the love our veterans have had for it and for us. All for which America stands is safe today because brave men and women have been ready to face the fire at freedom's front.'*
>
> Ronald Reagan

Anaphora

This is the repetition of a word or phrase at the beginning of successive sentences phrases or clauses. It is a powerful way of increasing impact.

Examples

'We shall fight on the beaches,
we shall fight on the landing grounds,
we shall fight in the fields and in the streets.'

Winston Churchill

'This royal throne of kings, this sceptred isle,
This earth of majesty, this seat of Mars,
This other Eden, demi-paradise,
This fortress built by Nature for herself.'

William Shakespeare

'What we need in the United States is not division. What
we need in the United States is not hatred. What we need
in the United States is not violence and lawlessness; but is
love and wisdom and compassion toward one another, and
a feeling of justice toward those who still suffer within our
country whether they be white or whether they be black.'

Robert F. Kennedy on the death of Martin Luther King

Antistrophe

This is repetition of the same word or phrase at the end of successive clauses. It is another powerful way of increasing impact that is seldom used these days but is very effective when implemented.

Examples

'In 1931, ten years ago, Japan invaded Manchukuo –
without warning. In 1935, Italy invaded Ethiopia – without
warning. In 1938, Hitler occupied Austria – without
warning. In 1939, Hitler invaded Czechoslovakia – without
warning. Later in 1939, Hitler invaded Poland – without
warning. And now Japan has attacked Malaya and
Thailand – and the United States – without warning.'

Franklin D. Roosevelt

'What lies behind us and what lies before us are tiny compared to what lies within us.'

Ralph Waldo Emerson

'... and that government of the people, by the people, for the people shall not perish from the earth.'

Abraham Lincoln

Assonance

This is the repetition of the same vowel sound in words to create rhyming or rhythm. It can help emphasis and memorabiliity

Example

'How now brown cow.'

'The rain in Spain falls mainly on the plain.'

'The gloves didn't fit. If it doesn't fit, you must acquit.'

Johnny Cochran, concluding arguments in the O.J. Simpson trial

Metaphor

This is an implied comparison achieved through the figurative use of words.

Example

'All the world's a stage,
And all the men and women merely players;
They have their exits and their entrances.'

William Shakespeare

'An iron curtain has descended across the continent.'

Winston Churchill

'No man is an island.'

John Donne

Personification

This is giving a personality to an impersonal object or thing. It can help bring ideas to life and help an audience relate to ideas or arguments.

Example

'England expects every man to do his duty.'

Lord Nelson

'Art is a jealous mistress and, if a man have a genius for painting, poetry, music, architecture, or philosophy, he makes a bad husband, and an ill provider.'

Ralph Waldo Emerson

'O beware, my lord, of jealousy!
It is the green-ey'd monster which doth mock
The meat it feeds on.'

William Shakespeare

Emphasis

When writing for the written word we can use exclamation marks to emphasize a point. But for the spoken word there are better techniques. Using the natural rhythm of sentences can be very effective if we remember that the end of a sentence has the most impact, followed by the beginning of a sentence. So put the most important points at the end and at the beginning of your sentences: that way your audience will remember them.

Repetition

Repetition lets you drive home a point or idea by making the audience pay attention. Martin Luther King's 'I have a dream' speech is a great example of this.

The rule of three

This is also called triplets or tricolon. It's a very simple and effective technique. You say something three times. Because, for some reason, lists of things, reasons, examples, whatever, all tend to come across with more impact when there are three of them. Things that come in threes are somehow more satisfying. Remember we said that three is a magic number? President Clinton used this technique a lot, as did Tony Blair when Prime Minister, and many other leaders.

Examples

'There are three kinds of lies: lies, damned lies, and statistics.'

Benjamin Disraeli

'May all of you as Americans never forget your heroic origins, never fail to seek divine guidance and never lose your natural, God-given optimism.'

Ronald Reagan

'Education, Education, Education.'

Tony Blair

Passive or active voice

When preparing and writing your speech or presentation it's worth following the example of Clinton by trying to use an active voice rather than a passive voice whenever your can. An active voice makes a speech easier to understand. For example: Having said that there may well be times when a passive voice is preferable.

- Active voice – 'The Sex Pistols released *Anarchy in the UK* in 1976.'
- Passive voice – '*Anarchy in the UK* was released in 1976.'

Clichés and jargon

These quite simply should be avoided at all costs. Unless they are being used for reasons of humour, which itself should be used intelligently, carefully and sparingly.

Key points

- Learn some techniques of rhetoric but don't overuse them.
- The rule of three is always worth using, but again not to excess.
- Repetition, alliteration and emphasis are useful tools to employ.
- An active voice is a more powerful and understandable voice than a passive voice.

To do: Bring it to life

Rewrite *The Rooster Prince* story as if you are going to read it to a group. Use the following techniques to give it more impact:

- the rule of three,
- repetition, alliteration and emphasis,
- active voice not passive voice.

'If any man wish to write a clear style let him first be clear in his thoughts...'

Johann Wolfgang von Goethe

'... the faculty of discovering in any particular case all of the available means of persuasion.'

Aristotle on rhetoric

10

the 50-word story and the 50-word review

In this part on the story element of The Clinton Factor we've covered:

- the power of story;
- the importance of structure especially the three-act structure;
- why we should always edit ruthlessly;
- making our story interesting and how we can bring it to life;
- rhetoric and writing techniques to give our story impact.

Let's now see if we can put them all together in some final exercises that reinforce all these points.

The 50-word story

The idea behind a 50-word story is very, very simple. You have to write a story in exactly 50 words. It can't be longer or shorter than 50 words. This probably sounds a very straightforward and easy task, but it can be surprisingly difficult to do well if you don't put into practice what you've been learning.

Your story must be a complete story – with a beginning, a middle and end. The title doesn't count and hyphenated words count as one word.

You can choose from the following exercises.

1 Write *The Hare and the Tortoise* or *The Rooster Prince* in 50 words without losing any of the meaning of the story.
2 Write your life story up to the present.
3 Write about what happened yesterday.

Give yourself a reasonable amount of time to achieve your target and then assess how well you did.

To do: The 50-word review

If you found the 50-word story exercise useful you may like to try these tasks.

- Write a review of a film you really loved in no more than 50 words.
- Write a review of a film you didn't like in no more than 50 words.
- Write a review of a book in no more than 50 words.

You can see real examples of 50 word reviews at www.50wordreview.com

---

The last word on story

The last sentence in *My Life*, Bill Clinton's autobiography, reads:

> *'As I said, I think it's a good story, and I've had a good time telling it.'*

part

status

three

In this part you will learn:

- that status is the bedrock to every piece of communication you have
- how to use status in your public addresses
- how adopting the right level of status will have a positive effect on all areas of your life.

what is status?

The kind of status we are talking about has little to do with positions of authority or social standing. Status is about how we perceive people and how we are perceived regardless of position or hierarchy.

Self-esteem

Does status have anything to do with self-esteem? Well, perhaps – but self-esteem is really about how we feel about ourselves rather than how we are perceived by others. Whilst we acknowledge that certain overlaps can be found between self-esteem and status the two should not be confused. We can all demonstrate characteristics of low or high status without suffering from low or high self-esteem – there is a big difference.

The three questions

Status is about the conscious effect we have on others and the conscious or sub-conscious effect others have on us. In Chapter 1 we spoke about the three sub-conscious questions we ask ourselves when meeting someone for the first time:

1 What sex is that person?
2 How old are they?
3 What is their status?

We cannot help but ask these questions. The first two questions do, of course, have a bearing on how we react to that person but the question about status will, whether we know it at the time or not, end up being the most important of the three. What is that person's status? What is that person's status compared to mine? Is it higher or lower? Is it similar? What kind of effect are they going to have on me? How should I behave with them? How do I play this person? All valid questions and all asked subconsciously.

Low status manipulation

After running a status workshop for an eminent record company during which we focused on the extremes of status and how to be wary of status abuse, we had a call from their head of training and development who had attended the workshop. She had an amusing tale to tell. Only a matter of days after our visit she there was a knock on her door. One of her staff wanted a word. Rather than entering the office and sitting opposite her boss, she decided to walk round the desk and crouch down next to her. She cocked her head on one side and looked up at her boss with 'cow eyes'. The boss stood up, pulled the girl to her feet and led her to the office sofa. They sat on the same level as each other and the boss asked the girl what it was she wanted. After a brief conversation the girl's request was denied and she left the room. The head of training believed she was being set up as a victim of low status manipulation and had she not recognized the tactic she may well have granted an unrealistic request.

Low status abuse

Is it possible to fall victim to a low status abuser? Does low status abuse exist? Yes it does and it's much more subtle and sinister than its high status counterpart. Low status abuse is devious and manipulative. Unlike its brash opposite it can be difficult to detect and even more deadly. Low status abuse does not manifest itself organically; it is cunningly acquired and cynically practised for personal gain. Low status abusers are not prone to unabashed outbursts like their conflicting opponents. Instead they wait patiently for an opportune moment when the victim's guard is down before inflicting their lethal sting.

We have all experienced a low status bashing with phrases like: 'Oh, you're so clever you – you're brilliant – I wish I could be like you – no really you are – you are brilliant – I could never do anything like that – aren't you clever – isn't she clever everyone?....' Aggggghhh! Go away!

Deliberate self-deprecation and the bolstering of others are the low status abuser's chief weapons. With carefully chosen words that ruefully run the speaker down and wistfully praise others the low status abuser moves in for the kill. The really skilful low status abuser will achieve their objective without their victim even noticing they've been had.

We've all encountered someone who makes us want to them put down. The kind of person who cringes around us, who is coweringly sweet, who irritates the heck out of us with this self-imposed subjugation, and if we challenge this person or level criticism at them, we're the big bad wolf. We are the ones that everyone will look sideways at for the rest of the day and the low status manipulator has got us again! Watch out – it's subtle but deadly. This kind of low status strategy destroys our ability to communicate properly and is best tackled by canny middle status intervention.

High status abuse

High status behaviour is usually quite blatant and in your face. It is frequently used to intimidate and bully, and is often adopted by people who don't actually want to communicate properly in case they might be wrong. People with narcissistic personality disorders often assume a higher level of status because it reinforces their love of themselves and their belief that it is everybody else who is out of step.

In a recent interview, author and actor Stephen Fry was speaking of responsibility when he said: 'duty, obligation, responsibility are all words that I have fought against all my life... if you feel you are doing something through responsibility – don't do it – but do project how you might feel if you don't do it... reneging on my word would make me deeply unhappy.'

That kind of sentiment would probably never enter the head of an extremely high status person because they would not care if they let other people down. Even worse they might wish their behaviour to have a harmful effect on those around them. Some high status people actually get a perverse pleasure from subjecting others to this kind of status abuse. This kind of behaviour is the antithesis of good communication and will have a negative impact on those around the abuser and affect company success. Fear does not equal respect. The only way to counteract behaviour like this is through middle status, 5 to 7 level Clinton behaviour. If we engage high with high, a long and bloody war of attrition will ensue with no winner. It is difficult to take offence at middle status and its undeniable strength. Finally, never be afraid of high level status – high status abusers are like animals that smell fear and pounce!

Marking out the territory

Animalistic behaviour with high status abusers is quite common. One particularly high status individual we coached displayed some typical territorial tendencies. On entering the room for an initial meeting he rearranged every single piece of furniture including the hat stand and the waste paper basket before sitting down. He might as well have peed up every wall! Levels 5 to 7 will do the trick. At worst the high status abuser will get frustrated with middle status and at best they will adjust their level of status to communicate in a less arrogant way. Either way the effect will be more positive than negative.

Give and take

We should never feel the need to prove our status and we should never claim status, as it will make us look insecure. This is, of course, the classic error of the high status abuser. We should also never try to take status. Saddam Hussein took it and therefore had it to lose. Let's think of a memorable image of Saddam Hussein, one that was shown several times on TV. Saddam on the balcony in his hunting tweeds, chest puffed out watching the troops parade past, shotgun in hand, firing off the shotgun. It doesn't get much more high status than that. Now let's think of other images: the image of Saddam being pulled out of a hole in the ground, the image of Saddam being photographed in his underpants, the image of someone poking around in his mouth with their fingers. Was he high status then? No way.

When there is a dramatic change in a person's status it is invariably from high to low.

> 'If I were married to her, I'd be sure to have the dinner ready when she got home.'
>
> George Shultz (American Secretary of State) on Margaret Thatcher

Margaret Thatcher was in a high status position as Prime Minister. She was also naturally a fairly high status person who played high status. When the men in grey suits came to visit, however, and she had to leave Number 10, had to walk to her car in tears, her status had crumbled. This dramatic change in status never seems to happen the other way.

The law of the jungle

Extreme low status can be equally as negative and unproductive. If someone has closed off in this way, either in business or socially, how can we communicate with them and move forward? It's virtually impossible. These people often fall prey to the high status abusers – just like the weak and vulnerable wildebeest gets picked off by the lions. The high status way of addressing the low status would be to bark such things as 'pull yourself together!' and 'speak up!' Adopting an equally low level of status to communicate would only result in a self-debasement contest. Again it is the middle level of status that stands the best chance of getting through. Being open, warm and approachable will allow the low status access to communicate. It defuses any fear of rebuke. It demonstrates a willingness to engage in a receptive and positive manner and serves to open channels of communication that can only impact in a good way. Low status individuals can only begin to operate and up their level of status if they are not in fear of reproach or high expectations. Only a middle level of status can give them the opportunity to communicate effectively. If this is practised the low status individual stands a good chance of functioning in the middle level of status: 5 to 7 every time!

Stick to the middle

The middle ground of status is unquestionably the way to go. We said that this is about social skills and that's true but we need to acknowledge that the right level of status is the absolute bedrock for good communication skills in every area of our lives. Once we assume that we are better or worse than other people we are heading down the wrong track. We must put ourselves in a position of recognizing the value of others without backing down or fronting up. The moment we inhabit a status below the 5 to 7 mark, we are in danger of being subjugated. If we try to establish a high level of status we will never be at an advantage. It's about respect. It's about being sensitive to the needs of other people. If we want to communicate effectively we must learn to listen and respond. We must only feel free to ask the things that will benefit others or at least be of mutual benefit.

Mine all mine!

Bill Clinton's level of status in his communications always gives a great sense of sharing. When George Walker Bush took office he looked like he owned the Oval Office, the White House and Air Force One. When Bill Clinton was in power, he appeared to take ownership of those things on behalf of the American people.

Stick to the middle of the road and avoid the murky mires on either side. There may be a number of Republican voters that would disagree with the opinion that this book has of Bill Clinton but let's look at the feelings and evidence both inside and outside of the United States. It may seem like a huge generalization but we feel that it's fairly safe to say that Bill Clinton is one of the all-time popular former presidents. This just goes to show that power and popularity can be achieved through middle status. In fact it is probably true that power and popularity can only be achieved through middle level status. Throughout the centuries, history has thrown up countless powerful figures who have been severely lacking in popularity. To make your way to the top and be generally liked and admired takes a very special quality indeed – The Clinton Factor. It's simple! Why didn't we think of it before? Be like Bill and we'll be all right! Easier said than done, hey? Maybe not. It's far easier to negotiate our way through life with a middle ground status than with anything either side of it. It's much simpler to let people in than cut them off. It's feels a lot better to give and get back rather than to keep and not receive. It's that simple!

The menace in the middle

Although the middle channel is definitely where we want to be, there is a rather nasty infection of middle status that we must be on our guard for – manipulative middle. Don't worry too much about this; it's really easy to spot. Once spotted, however, keep a very close eye on it. The manipulative middle abusers are those who appear to be of a confident, open, middle status but are really crafty and two-faced. They will seem to be genuine, sincere and friendly on the surface but are actually overfriendly and contrived. They will shake you warmly by the hand, probably too warmly and for too long, look you in the eye, again for too long, use your first name several times in one sentence having only just met you, and touch you in a patronizing kind of way. It is almost certain that these people will look for an opportunity of selling you down the river at some stage in your relationship and then hold out their open palms claiming to be innocent and hurt. Beware!

What a wonderful world

If everyone in the world were to adopt a middle level of status overnight, if we all decided to operate in that 5 to 7 channel of status, the Clinton channel, when we woke up the next morning, the world would be an amazingly pleasant place in which to live. Relationships would blossom, peace treaties would be signed, the greenhouse affect might be arrested, the hungry would be fed and the world economy would flourish. But life's not like that is it? But do you know what? We can go a long way to improving our lives and the lives of others simply by adjusting our level of status.

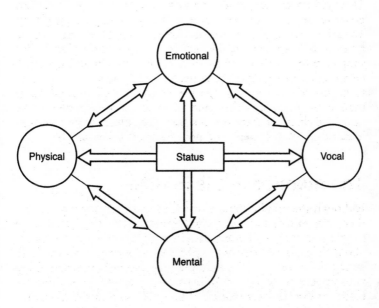

12

physical status

Many famous orators through the centuries paid great attention to physical fitness. When Cicero went to Rhodes to study under Apollonius Molon, his tutor subjected him to a fitness programme that would make many of today's athletes buckle. 'Speaking in the Forum is comparable to running in a race. It requires stamina and strength,' said Molon. Fortunately, today we have technology to support us. Had Rome's Forum been 'miked up', Cicero may not have felt compelled to stay in such great condition.

The right look

'It is only the shallow people who do not judge by appearances.'

Oscar Wilde

How we look is important but what we don't want to do in this chapter is to get hung up on clothing, cosmetics, weight, etc. What matters here is how our inner feelings and intentions affect how we are perceived physically. Let's remember that because people see our bodies long before we make eye contact it is our physical status that makes the first impression. Someone once said that we don't get a second chance at a first impression. We know that's a bit corny but it has its point. The last thing we want when meeting someone for the first time is to send out the wrong signals physically and then have to play catch up. We don't want people to feel overawed and we don't want to give others the impression that we could be a bit of a push over either. So, let's adopt a failsafe physical status that will support us throughout virtually every situation we are likely to find ourselves in – middle ground status, that 5 to 7 channel on the 1 to 10 Clinton factor scale. Later in this chapter is a checklist that keeps us in touch with the best level of physical status.

Comfortable – not arrogant

'When you're as great as I am, it's hard to be humble.'

Muhammed Ali (attrib.)

A proud, confident, straight, relaxed and centred posture will send out the right signals. It will make us more attractive. It will let people know that we mean business in the nicest possible way. It will make others take us seriously but not be afraid to approach. It's the Clinton level. Creating the right physical impression is absolutely crucial to getting a relationship off on the right foot. We need people to be interested in us before they know very much about us. We need to send out a message through our physical status that we are accessible and strong; that people can feel confident about establishing a bond with us. The signals may be silent but the way we carry ourselves has a profound impact on people we may want to cultivate or influence.

If we think about Bill's physical status probably the first thing that springs to mind is his height. Yes, he is a tall man and fairly well built too. One might think that his physicality is imposing and possibly even intimidating. Imposing yes – intimidating no. Bill Clinton has exactly the right level of physical status. He is fortunate that height is on his side. He neither apologizes for that nor does he use it to gain unfair advantage. He has adopted a level of physical status that shouts confidence and accessibility. If he were to play physical high status he would be pushing people away from him and as a politician he knows that would be a barrier to good communication. The middle ground physical status he assumes actually gives others the feeling that they can approach him and feel comfortable in his presence.

The Napoleon complex

A certain self-made businessman, who shall remain nameless, remarkably came to us for presentation coaching. (We say remarkably because it was quite clear that this particular individual had narcissistic tendencies so it was a wonder that he felt he needed any help in the first place.) He made an extraordinary statement – he said: 'If I'd been taller I would have been even more successful than I am now'. No, mister, if you'd been less bent on world domination and adopted a middle ground status, treating people with the respect they deserved you'd be even more successful than you are now! This person was short in stature but that certainly wasn't his problem. His problem was the pompous, arrogant, high-handed way he conducted himself in life. He did have a great degree of success in business but was an abject failure where popularity was concerned. None of us want to be like that. Did Napoleon have a thing about his height or did he just have a big horse?

We cannot stress enough how important it is to get the right level of physical status. It might seem obvious for athletes to pay great attention to their physicality but we should all be doing the same. If we get our status level wrong we will be putting ourselves at a disadvantage from the word go and have the devil's own job getting back to a decent starting point. Working with the right level of physical status is a communication skill that needs to be developed together with every other communication skill to create a great all round performance. The body can transmit a wide variety of feelings, attitudes and emotions and it needs to have a neutral base from which to operate. The body is a vital component to great communication and it is the first thing to come under scrutiny, so let's get it right. Once we understand the fundamentals of physical status we will no longer be at a disadvantage when communicating. If we don't understand the subtleties of physical status we will not have an insight into the intentions of others.

In the following sections we will map out what we believe is the best physical starting point as a platform for great communication. Once we have understood and achieved the right level of physical status great benefits will ensue. Not only will people communicate more readily with us, there will be an increased desire for others to join our company. We will feel physically better and more confident. We will have better balance and move in a more even and fluid way. We might even eradicate certain dull aches and pains that we have been carrying around for years. We will feel more relaxed. We will think more clearly. We will be more alert. People will be warmer and friendlier towards us. We might even begin to get our own way more often. We will feel better about ourselves and we will appear more attractive to those around us. Sound good? Of course it does. Read on!

Evolution

Man wasn't designed to stand upright and walk on two feet. We would all be much more comfortable if we were running around on all fours. Maybe evolution from the more hirsute primates was not the best thing that could have happened to man. Biologists and physicians will tell us that our frames just aren't up to the job of standing and travelling in a vertical manner. Even after centuries of evolution we are still not getting this standing up thing right, and back problems probably account for more sick time throughout the western world than any other ailment. We are, nevertheless, stuck with the vertical so we might as well make the best of a bad job.

Physical checklist

There is a very simple posture that provides the correct level of physical status for us to enjoy healthy and effective communication. This posture will, when one is used to it, be the most comfortable physical starting point for almost all activity. Let's take a look at the checklist:

1 Feet parallel, placed shoulder width apart.
2 Legs straight without knees being locked.
3 Pelvis tucked underneath spine – i.e. in a direct line with the spine (our bottoms will always stick out a small amount).
4 Arms hanging loosely by sides.
5 Hands and fingers relaxed.
6 Shoulders relaxed and level.
7 Neck straight and in line with the spine.
8 Head sitting perfectly straight on shoulders (check chin is not pointing up with head tilting backwards; check chin is not sitting on chest with head lolling forwards) facing straight ahead.

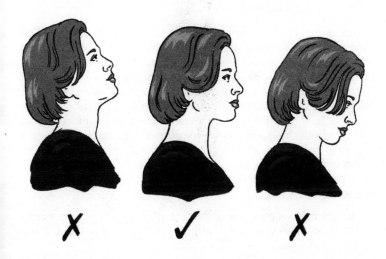

We mentioned Bill Clinton's height and its possible advantage to him but it is not necessary to be tall to stand a better chance at success. Napoleon Bonaparte had a fair modicum of success and he was short. We have all heard the expression 'Walk tall'. We have another version of that which is called 'being centred'. In order for us to send out the right physical signals for good communication we do not have to stretch our spines or try to lift our heads off our shoulders. The mid-level of physical status (being centred) can be achieved simply by standing erect with the head perfectly centred on level, relaxed shoulders. It really is as simple as that. This status level will send a positive signal across a room before facial expressions can be detected or eye contact established. It is absolutely crucial to start things off on the right foot. We must always remember that our physicality can say a lot about our state of mind and that people will make sub-conscious judgements about our character simply from looking at our posture. We need to come across as comfortable and confident so that others will wish to interact with us: 5 to 7 every time.

Being centred

When actors train the first thing to be examined is posture. This doesn't mean walking around the room with books balanced precariously on heads – that is probably best left to Swiss finishing schools. It's a matter of finding one's centre and understanding where that centre is at any point in whatever element of communication you are undertaking. Only when an actor is fully familiar with their centre can they begin to explore other physicalities. In order to play a character that has a physical deformity, an actor must have a neutral base to work from and be able to move from that comfortable base to the posture of the character they are playing with reasonable ease. Here are a few examples:

- Sir John Mills gave a brilliant Oscar-winning performance as Michael the 'village fool' with a facial and physical deformity in David Lean's *Ryan's Daughter*.
- Charles Lawton was probably the first screen *Hunchback of Notre Dame*. Daniel Day Lewis adopted an extraordinary twisted posture for his rather heart-rending performance in *My Left Foot*.

- On stage Antony Sher's portrayal of *Richard III* was a classic. (His book *The Year of the King* gives us an insight into his technique.)

None of these actors could have achieved these brilliant physical performances if they had not been centred in the first place.

Body language

There have been so many excellent books written on body language that all we want to do here is to make you aware of the physical extremes you need to avoid and look out for in others. The person in the diagram below may look confident at first glance but he is actually sending out some very negative signals. This is high physical status.

Head leaning backwards slightly to one side supported by hands. Body tilting backwards. Ankle resting on knee. It all sounds quite innocent but it is actually an open physicality that suggests over-confidence, arrogance and disinterest, and is almost aggressive and dismissive. The openness of this posture is quite contradictory in that the person is anything but accessible – they are actually pushing others away.

Let's take a look at the other extreme – low physical status.

Head bowed slightly to one side. Shoulders a little hunched. Almost stooping posture. Eyes looking at the floor. Fingertips barely connecting. This posture is saying 'please don't notice me – I'm not really here'. This classic example of low physical status has closed the person down, which will restrict any form of communication.

Let's put the two diagrams together.

Ouch! This really is not pleasant. This looks like subjugation. It is a picture we all recognize and find distasteful. You may feel that we are being over-dramatic but this is exactly what these images convey when they are put together.

Let's not go there

Best to stay centred at all times. You will not be dominating and you will not be physically undermined. We are in 5 to 7 land again: Clinton land. It's a good place to live.

A few tips

- When talking with your partner or children, check your physical status – what is it saying?
- When out shopping, check your status level with the salesperson assisting you.
- Ensure that you have the same mid-level physical status with your boss and the person beneath you.
- Keep a mid-level status in any social gathering and see the effect it may have on those around you.
- Mid-level physical status will make you feel and look confident and in control. Keep a check on it!

13

vocal status

'He has occasional flashes of silence that make his conversation perfectly delightful.'

The Rev. Sydney Smith on Thomas Babington Macaulay

If we were to say, 'It's not what you say – it's how you say it' we would be contradicting everything we said about story at the beginning of this book. What we say is very important. Getting the story right is crucial. It is also vital that we tell our story well and give it life. If we do not pay attention to the way we sound we will not achieve this. When we tell stories to our children we do all sorts of things with our voices that we would never dream of doing for an adult audience – what a shame!

Appearance isn't everything

So many people clearly do not pay any attention to the way they sound but if we were to ask them if they cared about how they sound they would all say, 'Yes, of course I do!' Then why are so many of us not doing anything to improve our vocal image? A great many of the people we are talking about have to stand and speak as part of their jobs and are probably much more concerned about how they look rather than what they sound like. It is very commendable that they are interested in their physical appearance but that is only one component of a total image. In fact, how people carry themselves physically can have an effect on their vocal image and vice versa – so let's get it right!

Today's technology brings so many facets to our everyday communication and it's important that we are able to embrace the galloping advancements and put them to good use. The great orators of centuries ago were not as lucky in that sense – they had to rely entirely on physical and vocal technique to get their message across. Let's think – is it really that different today? No, it's not. What is different is the degree of importance we give to maximizing our vocal impact by using technology. If anything we should be thinking of technology as merely assisting the hard work we put in on the sound we can make without artificial amplification.

Choice words

Neuro linguistic programming (NLP) practitioners will stress the importance of the words we select to communicate with and the effect they have on those around us. Isn't it interesting then, how many references we make to sound in our everyday communication?

- 'I hear what you're saying.'
- 'I don't like the sound of that.'
- 'The message was loud and clear.'
- 'We need to listen to ourselves.'

NLP will tell us that statements like these are sensory word selections. They are, of course, quite instinctive. As soon as we are born our contact with mother and the outside world is via smell, touch and sound. Even before we can actually focus on an object we start to communicate with sound – 'we find our voice' – we know that if we shout loud enough we'll get what we want. We grow up experimenting with sound. Sound becomes an enormous part of our lives. We learn by listening and we take our recreation by listening too. Why is it then that we stop paying attention to the way we sound? It seems crazy.

Put the work in

> *'The art of making deep sounds from the stomach sound like important messages from the brain.'*
>
> Winston Churchill

If we were to have a career in singing we would be training our voices on a daily basis, yet so many people who have to stand and deliver in their business lives do absolutely nothing about the way they sound. It's madness. A professional footballer will kick footballs every day even if there isn't a match next week. Pro golfers will hit balls into a net until their hands blister just to get their swing working well. They do it because their livelihoods depends on it. It is thought that managers in business will spend 80 per cent of their day communicating verbally. Isn't it then absolutely essential that they not only care about how they sound but that they do something to improve the way they sound? Of course it is!

Everyone knows that they can achieve more if *how* they say something has the 'right ring to it' (back to NLP). The voice is a very powerful and expressive instrument with a great range of sounds. We must never underestimate the power and control we can exert through our voice alone. Making a good first impression by getting our physical status right is very important.

Backing up that physical status by working on how we sound is just as important if not more so. We have all had the experience of 'good' or 'bad' teaching because of the quality and use of our teacher's voices. Teaching is certainly one profession where the importance of vocal delivery is paramount – teachers are, after all, helping to shape the lives of our children.

A lone voice

> 'Lord, what an organ is human speech when played on by a master.'
>
> Mark Twain

What happens when we are not able to use our physicality? What happens when we are not able to make that first impression through appearance and the effective use of body language? What happens when we cannot be seen? Many people earn their living being heard but not seen. Recording artists are the most obvious and the enjoyment of listening to them plays a huge part in our lives, but what about the announcers on TV and radio. What about the excitement created by the commentator on our favourite ball game or the frustration we suffer when we cannot understand what the man is telling us about the train on platform two? What happens every time we pick up the telephone?

There are countless thousands if not millions of businesses throughout the world that rely solely on telephone sales yet they appear to give absolutely no vocal training to their sales force. (They actually appear to care little or nothing about the content and their 'story' either but let's not go into that!) Have you ever had a bad experience at the hands of a company's switchboard operator? We know you have. How many times have you spoken to someone in business who couldn't give a damn whether you do business with them or not, or certainly sounded like they didn't? Plenty no doubt. Sound and vocal image is so important!

Cheer up it might never happen

We recently did some work for a rather prominent events organizer. Their automated telephone system ebulliently boasted that they were 'the organizers of the most exciting corporate events!' yet when you pressed 0 for an operator you might as well have been talking to Fred's Funeral Parlour! Some time ago we needed to make arrangements by phone to carry out some group work for a major automobile manufacturer. The voice on the end of the line was monotonous and appeared completely uninterested in what we needed to do. This was the voice of their director of communications! What on earth is going on? It simply isn't good enough! These people must be losing business hand over fist!

If the success of your company depends on great telephone technique, spend some money on training your staff to communicate the right company image. That means learning how to make the best use of your voice and at least sound vaguely interested in what you are doing! The difference between someone sounding bright, positive and happy to receive your call, and the negative, abrupt, couldn't care less approach, could be a customer hanging up and going elsewhere, taking a major contract with them. And it all started with the person who answered the phone!

Sounds good

All of this might sound obvious but so many businesses are getting it wrong. It is quite possible for a company to bumble along for years doing 'okay' when they should probably be doing really well. This could be down to how the company promotes itself generally or, equally, it might be due to the attitude and sound of the person on reception. Either way, those people managing the company need to look at the vocal image projected by those they employ. It's not difficult and it's worth investing in.

Getting the right level of vocal status and projecting a good vocal image is equally important in our private lives. The sound we make when talking to our partner or our children can mean the difference between enjoying peace and harmony, or living in an atmosphere of knife-edge tension. It really is as basic as that. The more we think about the effect our voice is having on other people, the more capable we will be at creating a productive and pleasant environment to live in. So, wouldn't it be great if not only our career prospects looked good but our love lives were also flourishing because we had found an understanding of vocal status and improved our vocal image. We must also remind ourselves that a good vocal image will count for nothing if we have not learnt to listen properly. Great communication is about listening and responding – the Clinton way.

High vocal status

'He loves the sound of his own voice!' How many times have we heard that?

There are those who talk '19 to the dozen' and appear to have a lot to say for themselves but could not be considered high status. There are also those who raise their chins and pontificate or simply 'talk down their noses' at us. Never quite sure which is more irritating? There are so many phrases that apply directly to high vocal status:

- 'You can hear her a mile away.'
- 'He's full of hot air.'
- 'Her bark's worse than her bite.'
- 'He's such an old wind bag!'

If we thought those kind of remarks were being said about us, we would, of course, be mortified. People would not only find what we have to say a turn off but they would also find the way we said it unpalatable and irritating – and they'd probably be right.

Pompous bluster, arrogant rhetoric, high volume righteous reproach, are all accompanied by tones of self-adoration. They are not attractive and they are counterproductive. It's not big, it's not clever but it can be quite funny. People who operate this high vocal status are often ridiculed and made figures of fun. If we look at some well-known situation comedies we can see how writers make great use of high status characters when writing their dialogue. Captain Mainwaring in *Dad's Army* and Basil Fawlty in *Fawlty Towers* are at their most comic when delivering their dialogue with bombastic pomposity. Both characters succeed as comic figures because of their high level of vocal status – anyone applying this in real life is sure to fail.

We were once asked to stand at the back of a room where a senior business figure was addressing a gathering of journalists to see if we could identify ways in which he could make his delivery 'even more dynamic' than it already was (his words apparently). The gentleman concerned went to great lengths to let his audience know that he wanted the meeting to be informal and that he would welcome any questions and comments they might have. Sure enough one journalist took him at his word and posed a question to which the 'dynamic' businessman barked back: 'This is a speech not a conversation!'

Needless to say, the remark and the ferocity with which it was delivered did him no favours and he was torn apart by the pack. What he said would have been a great line for Basil Fawlty or Captain Mainwaring and we would all have been quoting it with fondness for many years to come. But not quite as appropriate for a press conference.

The doctor will see you now

Some doctors' receptionists can dish out a nasty line in vocal high status. Many of us have been victims of the sharp tongues that separate us from the people who can save our lives and have, no doubt, changed surgery because of it. Why do people do it? It is so damaging and unnecessary, especially in this kind of situation where people are vulnerable and not at their best. Maybe being in positions of power where people can prey upon those at risk and in need of help attracts a certain type. Maybe there's a special training school for officious receptionists and PAs where they are taught to parry any innocent enquiries with vicious attacks. Who knows.

There is absolutely no room for high vocal status in good communication. Let's remember that certain forms of high vocal status are only a step away from physical violence. There are three ways in which high vocal status is dealt with:

1 Retreating and curling up into a ball for self-protection.
2 Bottling up the anger and eventually lashing out.
3 Meeting it with a neutral vocal status (more about that later).

It's perfectly safe to say that Bill Clinton does not employ a high vocal status. His vocal status, like his status in every other area of his persona, is in that 5 to 7 bracket. It's on the 7 end when emphasizing a point and possibly even a little higher than that when staunchly defending his position and the reputations of those close to him. It hovers around the 5 end when recounting a story with fondness or talking of the charitable causes he is involved with. It is without doubt the most failsafe and effective level to operate at.

Low vocal status

At the other end of the status scale is another no-no. We all make judgements about people because of the sounds they make and listening to low vocal status can be just as much as a turn off as having high vocal status inflicted upon us.

One could almost come down in favour of the high vocal status – well at least we can hear it! Sorry – that's a little facetious but you know what we mean. Of course low vocal status is not just about volume but being able to hear what someone is saying is pretty essential to good communication. In the same way that the volume of some high vocal status people can push us away, straining to catch what a person is saying will also have a negative effect. We are all by and large polite people and we will endeavour to make sure we listen to what a person has to say and respond accordingly. If the speaker is making it difficult for us to hear them, we will eventually become too embarrassed to ask them to repeat themselves again, give up trying to hear them and stop communicating altogether. Good communication must be fluid and low volume, low vocal status goes directly against that, closing us down. All sounds rather simplistic doesn't it? So why do we do it and why do we allow it to happen?

Don't sink to their level

Volume aside, there is another more disturbing manifestation of low vocal status which we all need to be aware of: low vocal status manipulation. Earlier on this book we spoke about low status manipulation and its dangers. Now we can pin-point and recognize the sounds it uses. The self-deprecating running down will invariably be done in whiney, almost hushed tones. The bolstering 'admiration' of others will be delivered at a slightly higher volume, in a simpering kind of way. Do not fall prey to this kind of assault (for that is what it is) because it will bleed you dry. It will sap you until your own status is heading down to join it. Beware!

Children are particularly good at low vocal status manipulation and many of them carry this strategy into their adult lives where it is performed with much less 'innocent' intentions. Cocking one's head to one side and speaking in a higher register voice is not cute in adults – it is done for a reason, which is devious and calculating. It is intended to catch you off guard and bring about an early capitulation. Children employ this tactic to obtain treats. The grown-up low vocal status abuser is playing for much higher stakes. When employing a child-like voice backfires, the speaker will simply come across as insecure and we will have no confidence in them.

When manipulative low vocal status is used in telephone conversations it can be particularly deadly. We don't have the benefit of reading the body language and that can make it more difficult to identify and tackle. It's always best to fight in the open where we can see what's happening. Dealing with this kind of approach on the phone can be a nightmare – yes, we could hang up but we're too nice for that so we continue the conversation at a disadvantage, being worn down bit by bit. Sound familiar?

So we must be in agreement that low vocal status is not for us. It is certainly not entertained by The Clinton Factor. If it were, we would definitely not have seen the rise to power of one of the world's most charismatic leaders. Let's stay in the 5 to 7 channel: the Clinton channel.

Mid-level vocal status: the Clinton level

'If you can talk with crowds and keep your virtue,
Or walk with kings – nor lose the common touch.'

Rudyard Kipling

Oh yes, this is the stuff! It's comfortable. It feels really good. It has the right effect and it fits perfectly with our mid-level physical status. No timid apologies and no deafening arrogance. We don't have to speak softly and we don't have to carry a big stick. We just have to listen and respond with a calm and measured thought and a clarity of speech at an acceptable volume. Easy! No, of course it's not that easy. Just like everything else in life we have to work at it, especially when we have probably paid it little or no attention at all. But it can be done and it will have an extremely positive impact on our lives and on the lives of those we come into contact with. Sounds ideal. Sounds impossible! Well let's take a look at some examples of mid-level status in action.

Carry on doctor

One of the great things about offering a service like ours is that anyone can use it and consequently we get the pleasure of working with a wide variety of people and professions. The Health Service and its employees are a great example of how effective mid-level status can be and, of course, how damaging adopting the wrong level of status can be when it comes to caring for people. We all know what a good and a bad bedside manner is – or do we?

Hitting the right level of vocal status when dealing with the sick is essential for speeding up their recovery and improving their well-being. Going for the Sir Lancelot Sprat approach as portrayed by James Robinson Justice in the film *Carry on Doctor* is unlikely to ingratiate any doctor to those in their care – patients cannot be intimidated into getting better. There are some doctors who will stand by the bedside speaking with a high vocal status to a group of trainee doctors about patients as if they weren't even there. By the same token a low status approach will not give a patient confidence in their doctor's abilities, which will add to their anxiety and possibly worsen their condition. Now we can see how important it is for people in the medical profession to get this status business right.

When talking to a good friend who also happens to be a general practitioner on this subject, he had an interesting theory about patient recovery. He believes that the body stands the best chance of working its own magic if a patient is comfortable and happy. Well, that certainly makes sense. Patients can only be comfortable and happy, however, if they are being treated with care and respect, and not being barked at or talked down to or having to strain to hear what is being said about them. We are talking about a good bedside manner: a mid-level status that listens and responds with a good vocal image. Our GP friend has no doubt that the way in which doctors communicate with their patients is equally as important as the treatment they give them.

Sound the alarm!

Fire fighters and paramedics tend to have the right level of status. Their vocal status has to be such that the people they are helping feel reassured and safe otherwise their jobs would be so much harder. They know that the people they are saving could go into shock at any moment and not recover so they have to instil in them a feeling of comfort and trust. Only a mid-level vocal status can achieve this. If the right level of vocal status can have the desired effect in these extreme circumstances, think what it could do for us in our everyday lives.

We mentioned teachers earlier in this chapter. One of our great experiences with the teaching profession has been with one of our coaches who is a teacher turned actor/director. In the 25 years we have know him we have never seen him outside of that 5 to 7 status bracket except when exploring status on stage. His talent and adopted level of status (especially vocal status) are a potent combination that equip him to get performances out of people that they never thought themselves capable of. He is a brilliant example of the positive effect that mid-level vocal status can have on those we have to connect with.

The scenery is better on the radio

Radio and TV presenters were also referred to earlier in this chapter but on radio the voice is the only instrument of communication they have. Two beacons of mid-level vocal status immediately spring to mind – John Humphreys and Terry Wogan. Humphreys' measured, urbane tonality assures the listener that they are in safe hands and Wogan's soft, mellifluous, dimple inducing banter has made him BBC Radio 2's favourite for over a quarter of a century. Both doing a brilliant job aided by middle-level vocal status.

Martin McGuiness, Sinn Féin leader, can never be forced out of his mid-level vocal status. Numerous political interviewers have tried to rattle McGuiness and push him over the edge but much to the frustration of many he has kept his composure and made camp firmly in that mid-level zone, which has made him a very effective communicator.

Fall in the men in Sergeant Wilson!

Bill Scully – an ex Special Forces serviceman, recently decorated with the Queen's Gallantry Medal for mounting a single-handed mission to rescue 1,400 tourists from the hands of blood-thirsty rebels in Sierra Leone (read his book *Once a Pilgrim*) – is a great example of mid-level vocal status. If you were to have a conversation with Scully you would never guess that he was a man capable of such an enormously heroic feat; he would simply be someone you felt drawn to and comfortable with. Colonel Tim Collins, now famous for his Shakespearean-style speech to his men at their camp in the Mayne desert just hours before they went into battle with the Iraqis, is another fantastic example of someone who has used his mid-level vocal status with great effect. Everything about Tim is 5 to 7 Clinton channel. When he speaks to audiences all over the world they understand why his men were willing to do anything he asked of them and why they had the utmost respect for the people they were engaging in battle. Here are two people who have had to work under very difficult conditions and achieved great things by staying in that mid-channel – they definitely have The Clinton Factor.

John McCarthy, the British journalist taken hostage in Beirut in April 1986, seems to inhabit that mid-level status area very comfortably. We can never imagine McCarthy getting on the high end of vocal status: it doesn't appear to fit with his character. This may well have stood him in good stead during more than five years of incarceration.

Let's do ourselves a favour and take a good look at our vocal image. Who knows – it might even save our lives one day.

Admirable Nelson

Nelson Mandela – one of the world's best loved political figures – is a wonderful exponent of mid-level vocal status. If there is anyone in the world entitled to have a serious attitude problem it is Nelson Mandela, but when he speaks we never feel that we are being lectured to or having a finger wagged at us. We see a man who appears comfortable with himself and happy with his life. We see someone we would feel very much at ease with. In spite of being wrongfully imprisoned for most of his life we simply see a man speaking passionately from his heart. It is interesting to note that Clinton is a very good friend of Mandela and visits South Africa every year for his birthday party.

Tackling low

Well, mid-level vocal status is definitely where we need to be. If we are dealing with someone who is employing low vocal status, whether it be in volume or tone, or even if it is trying to be manipulative, we need to stick rigidly to our mid-level vocal status. It's a secure anchor and it is very possible that we could, with persistence, raise the vocal status level of the person we are are engaging with and have a more meaningful interaction.

Tackling high

'Stop shouting at me!' The last we want to do when handling someone's extreme high vocal status is match them. Once again we need to hang on to our mid-level status come what may. This, will let the assailant know that you are not intimidated and that they need to drop their level or look silly. Honestly – it really works. Try it – you won't be disappointed.

The centre path

Mid-level vocal status will give you confidence, dignity and appeal. Don't even think of going anywhere else. Whether you are dealing with a difficult person at work, giving a public address or talking to the kids, it's where you need to be.

So, let's take a look at our vocal image as it is now and how we would like it to be.

PTSV – pitch, tone, speed, volume

Pitch

Let's not fool ourselves into thinking that we are suddenly going to have a voice like Richard Burton or Joanna Lumley. Instead let's develop our voices by finding our natural pitch. That means the pitch of voice we are most comfortable with. It will be somewhere in the middle of our range. Pitching it right is very important for our own comfort and very often our natural pitch is not the one we find ourselves using.

Some people seek to change the pitch of their voice (usually lowering it) to make themselves sound more sexy, appealing or authoritative. Margaret Thatcher did exactly this (to sound appealing) before she became Prime Minister – she lowered the pitch and softened her delivery. Do you really want to do that? If you do want to change the natural pitch of your voice, you need to ask yourself exactly why you want to change it and don't settle for anything other than a very valid reason. If you find a good reason then seek the help of a voice specialist. This book is not going to help those who wish to speak in a pitch that is an octave below the one that is natural to them; we are only interested in helping you to find the pitch that is most comfortable for you. We don't know if Bill Clinton has consciously changed the pitch of his voice but we would guess that he has not because it sounds comfortable and natural whereas, to us, Mrs Thatcher's never did. Keith Waterhouse once remarked that Thatcher always sounded as though she was talking to someone whose dog had just died. Maybe it's best to stick with what we've got!

Recognizing and strengthening our natural pitch will improve our everyday communication. It will also serve as a platform from which we can vary our pitch to emphasize certain points and give texture to our speaking voice. We really do believe that strengthening our natural game is the best way forward. We must also remember that the pitch of our voices will change naturally depending on how we feel about what we are saying. When it does vary naturally it will be supported with sufficient breath and our voices will be safe.

Stop thief!

If you were sitting at home and glanced out of the window to see someone stealing your car, you would probably shout 'Hey!!!!' at great volume and in a higher pitch than your natural speaking voice. When you are vocalizing naturally and instinctively, your breathing mechanism will support your voice automatically. If you decide to change the natural pitch of your voice without expert guidance, you run the risk of doing serious damage to your vocal chords. Be careful, our voices are our primary instrument of communication and they need to be cared for properly.

If we start to impose things falsely on our natural voice we will sound 'phoney'. As far as we are aware, the expression 'phoney' did not arise from the mistrust of what people were being told on the phone when they could not see the person they were talking to. Oh, we wish it did because it so precisely describes a trap we can all too easily fall into! Do we want to appear 'phoney'? No, of course not! So we must guard against using an unnatural voice. We won't be believed, even if we can be seen! We don't want that – it's a total turn off and people probably won't believe a word we are saying and who'd blame them? There is a suggestion that the origin of 'phoney' may be from the Irish *fainne*, a ring, from the old practice of tricking people into buying gilt rings which they believed to be genuine gold.

Everyone's voice is unique. Some people speak in a high register, others speak in a low register. Somewhere in the middle of the register will be your natural pitch. Once you have found your natural pitch you need only go 2 or 3 notes either side of that pitch for a more interesting delivery.

The exercises at the end of this chapter will help you find your natural pitch.

Tone

'Don't take that tone of voice with me!' Did your parents ever say that to you? Of course they did. The tone of our voices is extremely important for good communication. Choosing the right tone for the right situation can mean the difference of winning or losing, or life and death. Think back to the captivity of John McCarthy in Beirut. Remember the real life negotiators who hold people's lives in their hands. Getting the tone right is absolutely crucial.

Artists will use different tones of colour, like light and shade in a painting, to illustrate what they are seeing. We must use our voices like the artists use their palettes to tell our stories.

Tone is about resonance and intention. When our parents snapped at us for 'taking that tone' we had clearly upset them and maybe that was what we intended to do. The tones we choose to speak with are chosen to have an effect on those we are talking to.

People who use the extremes of vocal status tend to have tones that irritate us. The timid, slightly whiney tone of the low vocal status and the unpleasant, cocky tones of the high vocal status grate on the ears and make us unwilling listeners. A rather grand British actor taking the waters in a Wimbledon pub was overheard to say, 'No, darling, I turned the role down,. It wasn't my tonality.' The irritating tone of pompous arrogance. Yuk! High status at its worse. Let's hope his 'tonality' didn't appear too often on the stages of London.

God! He's so boring!

One tone that can operate at the high or low level is the dreaded monotone! Irritating vocal tones will make the listener switch off and the monotone is probably the worst of the bunch. People can be as enthusiastic as they wish about any subject on earth but if they have a monotonous voice they might as well keep quiet about it. Nobody wants to listen to monotones; they get on our nerves and even make us feel hostile to the person speaking.

Soon changed her tune

Your voice is such a powerful tool it can affect people in many ways and tone has a lot to do with it. This is why it is so important that we listen to ourselves and be selective about the tones we use for different situations. We also need to listen to the tones of other people that we find annoying and question if we use the same tones. If you think you do, then do something about it. Change your tones. It won't sound 'phoney' and it could improve or even save your life. The warm tones we choose to use within our natural pitch will make it easier for people to listen to us to get our message across and to make people want to communicate with us.

Let's remember how important getting the right tone is with some of the professions we mentioned earlier – the soldier, the nurse, the fire fighter, the paramedic, the negotiator – the success of these people is largely down to the tones they choose to communicate with and we should be just as aware about that fact as they are. There will be times when we need to step outside of the middle channel with our tones to achieve the desired effect but, by and large, the mid-level vocal status will serve us well.

Let's keep listening to ourselves.

Speed

The speed at which we speak is very important for good communication and once again the mid-level vocal pace is the winner. Some people speak very slowly which can make us switch off in frustration. We might even feel that we are being patronized by a slow delivery. We might feel that the speaker thinks that what they have to say is enormously interesting and that we will be hanging on their every word. We just want to receive the information more quickly so we can resume our usual pace of life. Whatever it is that makes someone speak overly slowly it almost invariably has a negative effect on the listener. Fortunately, it is only a very small percentage of people who speak too slowly – a much larger percentage of people speak too quickly.

She talks nineteen to the dozen

It's a strange expression but we know what it means. Machine gun fire speech can be just as frustrating for the listener as a laboured delivery but it is easier to understand why some people speak faster than we would like them to, especially when they are speaking in public and anxiety kicks in.

There are reasons other than anxiety for rapid speech. Some people have very fast and agile minds that jump around like grasshoppers. They are already on to the next bit before they've finished the bit they were doing. We must live in the now. We cannot expect our audience to keep up with us if we don't give them a chance – it's not fair and they will switch off. Once we understand why we are speaking too quickly we can do something about it.

We once worked with a very bright woman, who was head of HR for a major TV broadcaster and who was probably the fastest speaker we have ever encountered. It took some time to discover why she was like this but eventually we found out that she was the youngest of five sisters. When they were growing up personal speaking time was at a premium. She told us that when there was ever a gap in their conversation one of them had to jump in and get out what she wanted to say as quickly as possible before someone else took their turn. Of course she carried this into her adult life. Again, once we found out why she spoke so rapidly we were well on the way to curing the problem.

Errr...

Perhaps this is a good time to talk about audible pauses. The 'ums' and 'ers' that we pepper our speaking with. Not so bad in everyday conversation but in a speech or a presentation they are very irritating indeed. As soon as we understand why we do it we can do something about stopping it happening. We do it in conversation because we feel that we need to fill those gaps or someone else will jump in and take our turn at speaking. It's true! That's the reason – and it's sub-conscious. When we stand up to make a speech or a presentation we don't have that problem. Nobody is going to jump in unless they are invited to comment – they wouldn't dare! So instead of filling in the gaps with 'ums' and 'ers' leave them empty. Audible pauses are not attractive – real pauses are great and, believe it or not, it is very interesting watching someone who isn't speaking!

Back up to speed

We must speak at a pace our audience can keep up with which, for most of us, will mean slowing down to a pace that probably feels laboured, dull and uncomfortable. It won't come across as laboured or dull; it will almost certainly be just right. Get someone to listen to you speaking – ask their opinion of whether you are too quick or too slow. Once you have the pace that your audience can be comfortable with and absorb what you are telling them – then you can vary the pace, give light and shade to your delivery and make the way you present information and ideas more interesting.

Volume

The problem is like being too quick or too slow only this time it's too loud or too quiet.

There is a story of two rival actors at a friend's birthday party both with huge voices trading insults from different rooms. It was a long and bitter battle before one delivered the killer blow: 'Is it true you began your theatrical career in the circus where a lion had to put its head in your mouth?'

Can you hear me at the front?

'Get on, say the wordies loud and clear, and get off.'

Pamela Brown (actress)

The best place for booming theatrical voices is on the stage and certainly not in our everyday lives or business presentations. Although actors attempt to hold the mirror up to nature, they can, on occasions, let the play run away with them and 'over resonate'. Because the theatre situation is not a natural one we can forgive them and even enjoy a big performance. Some of today's younger actors have been criticized for mumbling on stage and not being heard. Sir Peter Hall who founded the Royal Shakespeare Company said recently: 'Actors now think that if they raise their voice, they are being "unrealistic". I tell them: "What you do is unreal. You're wearing someone else's clothes and speaking someone else's words'."

The same is not true in life outside the theatre and we must be conscious of the volume we use in our communications. We need our audiences to be comfortable with the volume of sound we are delivering.

Whenever we have any presentation skills training we will invariably be told to speak up. Yes, it is important that we can be heard but it is also important that we don't over do it. We must listen to ourselves and ask the opinion of others about how we speak. It is very unlikely that we will find ourselves in a situation where we are asked to speak without amplification but we do, nevertheless, need to produce sufficient volume for the microphone to pick up. If we deliver a muffled utterance, the mike will amplify and muffle the utterance further. Just like everyone else in the room, we will be able to hear and adjust the level of amplification if necessary. It's all about listening to ourselves.

The biggest danger, when it comes to volume, is not being heard. This occurs when low vocal status is in action, as mentioned before. If we cannot be heard we might as well not bother speaking at all. Yes, it really is as simple as that. There are a number of reasons why people find it difficult to make themselves heard and a lack of confidence in their ability to communicate is the main one. Confidence comes when all the components of good communication are working together as one – The Clinton Factor. We can be painfully shy but still operate as good communicators when we take the trouble to piece together the elements we need to connect effectively. The exercises at the end of this chapter will help you to find your voice and enjoy using it. Finding your natural speaking voice can be very empowering. Go for it!

The right vocal status

The right vocal status will make us accessible. The right vocal status will mirror everything that is good about the right level of physical status. What we really want to achieve by getting our vocal status where we need it to be is the desirability for others to communicate with us. That's all. If we achieve that people will listen to us and what we have to say might have a positive effect on them. What more can we ask? If we have that Clinton level of status – open warm, receptive, approachable and strong – every area of our lives will flourish. We won't be the canny businessperson who makes millions but whose family finds them difficult to connect with. We won't be the Mr or Mrs Nice Person who hides their light under a bushel and never gets what they want. We won't spend a miserable life avoiding speaking obligations. We will enjoy productive personal development. We will be more attractive to those around us. We will have opened the gate to a whole new world of positive personal interaction.

A painful experience

Very few people like the sound of their own voice. Those that do have almost certainly not bought this book anyway! There can be so many things that we don't like about our voices. We may whine, talk nasally, speak too softly, speak too loudly, mumble, have audible pauses and numerous other vocal tics. If you can bear it, record your voice and see what it is you don't like about it. Once you have identified what it is that you dislike you can start to do something about it. The following exercises are quite basic. They will help you to breathe properly and support the sound you make. They will also help to give you clarity and dexterity of speech. Have fun!

Breathing exercises

Before we begin to find the sound that is best for you, we need to look at some breathing exercises to ensure that you are correctly supporting the sound that you make with sufficient breath. The best way to understand how your breathing mechanism works is to start from a lying position. First, find a clear floor space, preferably carpeted or use a foam mat.

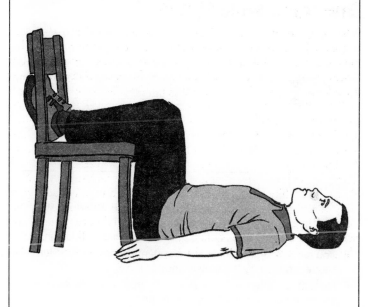

Lie on your back with your legs resting on a chair. The backs of your knees need to be in contact with the edge of the chair's seat so that your upper and lower legs form a right angle. This will help your spine to connect with the ground and you should be able to feel the small of your backs touching the ground. Your neck should be as straight and close to the ground as possible. Your shoulders need to be relaxed with arms lying straight by our sides with hands and fingers relaxed.

This is probably one of the most comfortable positions you are ever likely to find yourself in – enjoy. Many actors we know cat nap in this position in their dressing rooms in between shows and there is no reason why anyone else can't do the same – even in the office there's bound to be a quiet corner where you can recharge your batteries at lunchtime. Give it a go. It is also a great starting position for your breathing exercises. As you relax and release tension you will feel your back connecting with the floor as you expand your lungs.

Breathing technique

You will be breathing as deeply as possible during these exercises. Always breathe with the stomach and imagine breathing with the lower back. This will make sense when put it into practice and you feel the mechanism working. Do not snatch breaths from the top of the chest.

Spend plenty of time on these exercises – they are for relaxation and releasing tension. Try to do them just before going to bed – they will help to give you a good night's sleep.

Exercise 1

1 Breathe in for a count of 7 and release on an 'sssss' for a count of 10.
2 Repeat several times before increasing release counts in 5s.
3 You are looking for a fluid and constant release of air which can be determined by the consistency of the S sound.
4 Repeat as often as you like with breaks in between each exercise so you do not hyperventilate.

Exercise 2

1 Same as above but releasing on a 'shhhh' sound – this is not as easy.

Exercise 3

1 Same as above only in a centred standing position (as referred to in Chapter 12 on physical status).

Vocal exercises

Use breathing technique as described above.

Exercise 1

1 Breathe in for a count of 7 and release air for a count of 10 on a middle range hum where your voice is most comfortable.
2 Repeat this exercise several times before increasing release counts in 5s.

Exercise 2

1 Same as above but release air on a hum and open your mouth into an 'ahhhh' sound.
2 Repeat this exercise several times before increasing release counts in 5s.

Exercise 3

1 Hum slowly up and down through your range – when breaks and cracks are eliminated your voice is beginning to shape up.
2 Repeat the exercise several times.

Note: The Change of sound from 'hum' to 'ahhh' should be smooth and not staccato. When the humming sound is placed correctly you will feel a tingly sensation on your lips – this means that the voice is placed forward in the face where it should be. Be gentle with open sound at first, building it gradually, and take your time in between exercises so as not to hyperventilate. Make sure you do exercise 3 last when your voice is properly warmed up.

Speech and diction exercises

Start with the following warm up.

Jaw massage

1 Relax the lower jaw and gently massage the jaw hinge with your fingers, using a circular motion.

Jaw drops

1 Let the jaw drop open to the height of two fingers (a pretend gun in the mouth!).
2 Repeat several times.

Opening the sound

1 Let the jaw drop open to the width of two fingers.
2 Keeping the tongue in the floor of the mouth, sound the five vowels: aay – eee – aiy – ohh – uuu.

Then move on to some speech exercises.

Tongue twisters

To develop confidence and dexterity and to strengthen the tongue.

Ts

- A tidy tiger tied a tie tighter to tidy her tiny tail.
- A twin track tape recorder.

Ds

- Do drop in at Dewdrop Inn.
- Do daring deeds do damage?

Fs

- Five frantic fat frogs fled from fifty fierce fishes.
- Five fashionable females flying to France for fresh fashions.

Vs

- Violet vainly viewed the vast vacant vista.
- Vera valued the valley violets.

Ps

- Please Paul pause for applause.
- Peppercorn pudding and pelican pie.

- I want a proper cup of coffee made in a proper copper coffee pot. Tin coffee pots, iron coffee pots, they're no use to me. If I can't have a proper cup of coffee made in a proper copper coffee pot, I'll have a cup of tea!

Bs
- A big blue badly bleeding blister.
- A blue-backed blackbird blew big bubbles.

Cs
- A coster carried crates of cabbages across a crooked court.
- A cricket critic cricked his neck at a critical cricket match.

Gs
- Gertrude Gray gazed at the grey goose gaily.
- Greengages grow in greengage trees.

Rs
- Round and round the rugged rock the ragged rascal runs.
- Real roses rustle rurally.

Shs
- Shoppers shocking shopping, shocking shoppers shopping.
- Sheila's Shetland pony shied, shooting Sheila on the shore.

Ch's
- Cheryl's cheap chip shop sells cheap chips.
- Charlie chooses cheese and cherries.

Ths
- They threw three thick things.
- Three thrushes thrilled them.
- There are thirty thousand feathers on that there thrush's throat.
- A thin little boy picked six thick thistle sticks.
- Sir Cecil Thistlethwaite, the celebrated theological statistician.

Hs
- 'Hold him here!' hollered Harold.
- How high his highness holds his haughty head.
- He ate hot apples and halibut hastily.
- The hare's ears heard ere the hares heeded.

14

emotional status

'When things are steep remember to stay level headed.'

Horace, Roman Poet

The fundamental factor

Some time ago during one of our Speechworks staff training sessions we were stressing the importance of working with status when one of our coaches made an interesting observation. We were naturally keen to emphasize that all areas of status must be covered – physical, mental and vocal – but it was pointed out to us that we had failed to address emotional status. Is there such a thing? Doesn't that come into mental status?

Although our training day had only just started we spent the rest of the day discussing emotional status. Yes, not only does it exist but it is probably the most important area of the subject of status, and yes, it does fall into the mental category especially with regard to the management of emotion. It turned into a fascinating day of discovery. Emotional status is at the very core of all our communication, it is the inner-artist's palette, it is the tool that shapes The Clinton Factor. If we develop our emotional skills we are going to live happier and more successful lives. We will function with a greater clarity of thought and enjoy more productive relationships. We will operate with empathy and a better understanding of other people's needs. We will be able to stay focused on what is important in our working and personal lives. Emotional status is the key to the success of every piece of human interaction.

Emotional understanding

Understanding our own emotions gives us a greater insight into the moods and desires of other people and allows us to make the right decisions about how to react appropriately to them. Not only will it help us manage our own performance, it will also give us the ability to steer the behaviour of those around us and create win–win situations. Logically applied, management of emotions will equip us to make choices that will enrich our business, social and domestic lives.

Beware the dark side of the force!

At the risk of banging on about the extremes of status we do need to stress the dangers of operating under the 'dark side' or, indeed, the 'somewhat too light side' of the emotional spectrum. The outer limits will, of course, close us down for meaningful communication. Anger and rage are not agents of positive communication – they will only serve to push people away with no desire to resume normal service. Obsessive worrying is the route to an unattractive anxiety disorder. Over-enthusiastic, forever smiley behaviour will probably be considered glib or flippant and certainly not be taken seriously. Deeply sincere hand-holding concern will be greeted with mistrust. Neglecting to exercise some control over the extremes of emotion will get in the way of our ability to focus clearly on what we are doing.

> 'If you can keep your head while all around you are losing theirs…'
>
> Rudyard Kipling

Those people who are attuned to their emotions and who are able to manage the extremes recover from set backs far more quickly and are able to get on with enjoying their lives. We know that life in business is fraught with people problems, obstacles that need to be negotiated and rejections that must be coped with. People in sales can suffer rejection frequently and have to have techniques and strategies for dealing with that. Those that allow the emotional extremes that can result from rejection to set in are sure to be out-sold by the sales staff that are in command of their emotional status.

Bill Clinton is a man with a great intellect – that intellect would never have been able to operate efficiently if he had allowed it to be hijacked by emotional extremes. This was never more apparent than in the interview with Chris Wallace on Fox News Sunday when Wallace pressed Clinton on his handling of terrorist activity when he was in the White House. Although angry, Bill was able to restrain that emotion sufficiently in order to make his points in a clear but forceful manner.

Let's get this thing right! Again – not rocket science, so why do so many of us get it wrong so much of the time? Maybe we get it wrong because we have not been aware of how wonderful things can be when we concentrate on getting it right. Perhaps we get too tied up in ourselves to reap the benefits of understanding and focusing on the needs and desires of others.

The need for empathy

Empathy begins in infancy. Small children empathize naturally. We've all seen children cry because another child is crying. They are simply attuning to the feelings of the child in distress. They have made an emotional connection. It's instinctive – in order for children to be happy they need to be in an emotionally stable environment which extends to the feelings of other children around them. Children develop this skill quite naturally. As we get older, and our lives become more cluttered, we tend to lose some of this innate ability.

The bigger picture

We need to be empathic if we are going to be successful and only a clear understanding of our own emotions is going to allow that to happen. Emotions are good and without them life would be very dull indeed so let's not suppress them. We need to examine our feelings. We have to be sure that our feelings are real and not what we want them to be. We have to understand that what we feel at the moment isn't necessarily what we might feel in two minute's time. We need to check our feelings and make sure that they are true. When we can do this, we can recognize the true feelings of others and empathize with them.

Anyone who ignores the need for empathy and continues to bash down the road to their own success regardless of the feelings of other people will lose out because they are not seeing the bigger picture. It's important that we understand our emotions so we can be attuned to the feelings of those around us. Interpersonal understanding is the very cornerstone of a happy and successful life. It will maintain the balance needed to steer a true and harmonious course through our business, domestic and social lives.

There are plenty of good resources available to help you, but you may like to look at a companion book in the Teach Yourself series – *Emotional Intelligence* by Christine Wilding.

People skills

We've all heard about people skills – they are all about being empathic. If we are not sensitive to the feelings of others we do not have people skills. This is where Clinton scores so highly. He has the leadership qualities that are born out of genuine empathy. He has the ability to bring people together to resolve differences; an instinctive nose for the requirements and desires of other people; a capacity to listen and respond to the worries and concerns of those around him; and a capability to interpret the mood and react accordingly. This is what sets him apart from the rest. These are the emotional skills that make him one of the world's greatest communicators.

Stop bickering

We need to remember who it was that brought Arafat and Netanyahu to the same table at Camp David and who it was that played such an instrumental role in the Irish peace process. This is evidence of tremendous people skills on the world stage. These kinds of achievements simply don't happen to people who do not have a talent for empathy. Whether or nor Clinton likes the people he has to deal with or agrees with what they stand for is neither here nor there – what is important is his ability to read, understand and respond to them in a positive way and bring the opposing factions together.

We spoke earlier about the idea of everyone in the world waking up one morning with that mid-level status in every area and what would happen. Well, the above are examples of exactly what can happen at the highest level. It works! Caring, listening and reacting empathically are at the root of happier and more productive lives. We are all capable of it. We can all read the body language that gives away emotion – the look, the gesture, the posture, the tone of voice. We just need to take the time to access our own emotions and attune to the feelings of others.

Listen and share

If we think about the people we are drawn to, they are usually the ones in touch with and in control of their emotions. They are invariably the people who seem interested in us, listen well and make us feel good. They know what makes us tick and are able to press all our happy buttons. What a quality! It is hard to be jealous of these people – they are too easy to like – and do you know what? We can be just like them with a little application.

We must never forget that displays of emotion will always have an effect on other people so we must monitor ours and be ready to read and empathize with others. We all know people who always seem to be there for us, people we can rely on, people we trust, people who consider our feelings, people who listen! These are the people we gravitate to, these are the people we find attractive, these are the people we want to be with. They have charisma and the reason they have charisma is because they are accessible, in control and attuned to the needs of others – they share themselves with us and make us feel special. A lot of people may have this quality naturally but we are all capable of recognizing and developing it in ourselves.

Building a rapport

Knowing how other people are feeling helps us to create a rapport. Understanding and managing emotion in ourselves and others is a skill we need to learn and hone if we are going to improve life for ourselves and those we come into contact with. This is the skill of the leader bringing people together to work as one. This is the skill of the negotiator resolving the differences of warring factions or interacting with hostage takers. This is the skill of the good salesperson sensing what is right for the customer and building long-term relationships. This is the skill of the military commanders who are responsible for the lives of their troops. This is the skill of the nurse who understands what it takes to help a patient make a speedy recovery. These may seem obvious positions where good management of emotion is crucial but whatever we do and even when we are at home or out with friends we can all be more sensitive to our emotional status. Towards the end of this chapter there is a checklist to see how we can improve our interpersonal performance with regard to emotional status.

A good old weepy

When we are at the theatre or cinema we expect our emotions to be touched in some way by what we see on stage or screen. We are happy to let our guard down and give ourselves up to the whole gamut of the emotional spectrum; in fact we kind of expect to have our emotions pulled apart. Fear, anxiety, sadness, joy are all par for the course in that short period of time. It is the job of the actors to use their emotional skills to steer our emotional status. This conscious management of an audience's emotions is no different when making a speech or presenting a seminar.

Emotion at the podium

The moment we stand up to speak we have the opportunity to change the feelings of our audience by demonstrating how we feel about the subject we are speaking about. We must decide how we want our audience to feel when we have finished speaking. Their emotions are very much in our control. There is probably one overriding feeling that we must always leave our audiences feeling no matter what the subject – hope.

A politician's vision. The plea on behalf of a charitable organization. The heartfelt words of the bride's father. All of these examples of a speaker's subject matter should leave us with a sense of hope. A hope that if we vote for the speaker things will get better. A hope that our donation will give the starving food. A hope that the newly-weds will live happily ever after.

Hope throughout history

Hope seems to be an underlying theme in almost every form of public address and no more so than in practically all of the most famous speeches in history: Churchill's 'fight them on the beaches' speech. Martin Luther King's 'I have a dream' speech. Bill Clinton's acceptance speech for the Democrat's nomination. All laced with hope. Even some of the distasteful rallying addresses of the Third Reich were about hope. Hope is probably the best, almost failsafe, feeling to send an audience home with – it's positive, upbeat and optimistic. Leading up to the hopeful ending a speaker can evoke a whole series of different emotions taking an audience on a journey of ever-changing emotional status. Again, just like the theatre or cinema, it is what we expect from the experience, and the skill of the performer is in being able to move and influence an audience in this way, especially when spectators believe that they have witnessed the speaker's true feelings.

The great speakers of history from Demosthenes to JFK have been able to sense an audience's feelings and respond to them. The best communicators are those who are sensitive to the mood of the crowd. Caesar, Churchill, King, Hitler were all able to create and shape the emotional journey of their audiences. All of them honing and developing their craft with every speech. Even the great Roman orator Cicero saw the need to refine, rehearse and be trained in the art of speechmaking. Some of the greats were natural-born communicators but they also recognized the need to improve their skills. Those who have followed Bill Clinton's career say that he did not start out as one of the finest speakers of our time – he had to work at it. Once we are in tune with our emotions and the emotions of other people, and are prepared to put in the time, we too can obtain the power of a good speaker.

How sensitive are we?

'Good breeding consists of concealing how much we think of ourselves and how little with think of the other persons.'

Mark Twain

We need to monitor as many different pieces of communication as we can to see if we are managing our emotions and the emotional status of those in any given situation. Below is a checklist to help us out.

More listening

- Do we really listen to other people?
- Have we already decided how we are going to respond before listening to everything being said?
- Do we give ourselves the chance to understand fully another point of view by listening properly?
- Do we sometimes dismiss what others say (particularly children) because we consider them of inferior intellect?

- When we listen to other people are we considering how they are feeling when speaking?
- Do we really care what other people have to say? We should!

Social

- Do we shy away from meeting new people?
- Do we regard meeting new people as an interesting opportunity?
- Do we tend to stick with the people we know?
- Are we happy to break away from those we know and meet other people?
- Do we show a genuine interest in others?
- Do we ask interested but unintrusive questions of others?
- Do we remember peoples' names?

Business

- Have we decided the value of a colleagues's comments before properly listening to them?
- Do we view each new piece of communication as an opportunity for development?
- Are we sensitive to the feelings and concerns of those we work with?
- Do we take the trouble to find out about our colleagues' families?
- Do we take the trouble to find out what our colleagues' hobbies are?
- Are we genuinely interested in our colleagues' lives outside of work?
- Do we think of how we can assist our colleagues in their work?
- Do we take the time to spend a few minutes each day in informal chat?
- Do we really care about our colleagues' well-being? We Should!

Domestic

- Have we become too wrapped up in our own working lives to connect properly with our families?
- Do we give value to what our children have to say?
- Do we enquire about our partner's day first?
- Do we focus on what our partner has to say rather than looking for an opportunity to turn the conversation to ourselves?
- Do we take the time to find out what our children have been doing at school?
- Do we know the names of our children's friends and the names of their teachers?

I hear what you are saying

Getting the right emotional status is about being empathic. Empathy is about listening. Listening is about hearing what someone has to say, being interested in what they have said and remembering what they have said. It is no good just giving the impression of listening – what happens the next time you meet that person and you cannot remember a word they told you before? If we want to be liked and communicate effectively we must listen, respond and remember. Great salespeople will absorb information about their clients that some people would consider irrelevant but the next time they meet a client and ask how their daughter's wedding went or if they had a good holiday in Spain, they will be more likely to get the order than the person who has not digested that information. It's a personal touch and we all respond positively to someone who has taken an interest in us.

What's his name?

From what we hear about Bill Clinton it would appear that his interest in and empathy with others has played a major role in his success as a communicator. Clinton, apparently, is great at remembering people's names. It is very flattering when someone remembers who you are and can inspire great respect for those who, like Bill, do the remembering. It is also extremely tiresome when someone never remembers your name – in fact you are feel insulted and probably likely to avoid contact with that person in order not to let the situation connect with the extremes of your emotions.

When working on status with one particular client from a rather enormous organization, he related a story about when he was a young and lowly clerk working with a man who later went on to make it to the top. Several years later he saw the man again at a company function and congratulated him on his success within the company. Our client was most impressed that the man did not only remember him, his name and where he was working, but took time to indulge in some idle chit chat about how he was getting on and how his family were.

There is no doubt that emotional status and empathy are great contributors to The Clinton Factor.

15

mental status

'The brain is a wonderful organ. It starts working the moment you get up in the morning, and does not stop until you get into the office.'

Robert Frost

The brain is indeed a wonderful organ but it can sometimes take us in directions we should avoid. We need to be in the best frame of mind all day, every day if possible. It's not easy to be upbeat all the time – there are bound to be times when problems play on our minds and hold us back; it's only natural. Adopting the elements that make up The Clinton Factor should help us discover a mental status that will help us through difficult times and situations. The different areas of status we talk about in this book need to work together for maximum effect and having the right level of mental status is a key component in this process.

In the theatre if things do not work well on stage it is all too often down to a lack of attention to the status level of the characters in the play. Well, we are sure that the same can be said for how things work out for all of us in life. We need to be sure that we are applying the right level of status in every area of our performance for complete success. Getting our physical and vocal status right means being in a positive frame of mind and keeping in check extremes of emotional status. That way every bit of our performance engine can connect properly and run smoothly. The right mental status is the one that acknowledges the need to monitor constantly the other areas to make sure that we are getting the maximum performance from our status levels all the time. It's about being aware.

Beam me up Scottie!

There is one major concern that our calm and rational mental status must address when it comes to giving a good performance – anxiety:

- 'I hate this – let's get it over with as quickly as possible and get out of here.'
- 'These people aren't interested in what I'm saying – let's blast through it and go home.'
- 'The sooner I can get through this the better – then I can relax.'

Sound familiar? Anxiety when speaking in public is a subject that must be addressed as more and more of us have to make presentations as part of our working lives. So many of us are thrilled to get the job we want, alas, all too often without realizing that somewhere down the road standing up and making presentations is going to be a major part of the job. So, it's either spend a miserable life finding ways of avoiding it, look for another job or tackle anxiety. Most people are much better at standing up and speaking than they give themselves credit for but this does nothing to reduce their anxiety.

Some of the people that work for The Speechworks are professional actors who, perversely, put themselves through this kind of agony by choice and are used to being sick into fire buckets before going on stage. Naturally you would expect them to have some techniques and strategies for dealing with the world's number one fear. So, before rushing of for hypnotherapy or to seek the services of a specialist psychologist, let us make a few suggestions. Here is our five-point programme:

1 Always remember that the audience's well-being is the most important thing. The last thing an audience wants is to be nervous on behalf of the person speaking. They want to enjoy themselves. They are more important than you. They need to feel at ease. Your concerns should be for them not you. They want you to be good. It's not about you – it's about them, what they want and what they want to take away.

2 Feeling the part is very important. When actors step out on stage they are in costume. Their costume is an aid to their characterization – it is an integral part of their performance. Get a costume! Including shoes! Take someone with you! Don't step up there wearing what you had on yesterday – this is a special performance. Look good. Treat yourself to something you wouldn't normally wear to work. Get a new aftershave or perfume. Feel the part.

3 When the curtain rises on a play the actors are already in character. They have been warming up and preparing for the last 30 to 60 minutes. Start your performance early. When you have read this book and you understand the components that make up The Clinton Factor, put them together well before you stand up to speak. Be in character when you leave the house or when you walk through the doors at work in the morning. Start your performance early and when you begin your presentation you will already be half way through the show.

4 You are the expert. You are being asked to speak because you know your subject. What you have to offer your audience is gold dust. If you believe in your material it will support you. Have faith in your material and remember why it is you are standing up there speaking – you are the expert!

5 Try to embrace the artificiality of the situation. This is not an occasion where you are having an informal chat to a small group of people around a table in a bar. An audience always enjoys these unnatural situations. Perhaps we should recognize that and accept them for what they are. Help the audience to enjoy the artificiality even more. Play the part.

Take a good look at the vocal and breathing exercises in Chapter 13 on vocal status. These will help you to build a sound technical platform, which will raise you level of confidence and reduce your level of anxiety.

Help!

Earlier in this book we referred to the notion of being confident through preparedness. It is an irrefutable fact that the best cure for anxiety when speaking in public is to be thoroughly prepared. It means bringing the three principal components of The Clinton Factor into play: story, status and focus. We know that audiences enjoy the combination of SSF. We know that they address the primary concerns for good communication. We know that they work! A little dedication to the areas of story, status and focus will have a positive impact on your life as a speaker and your life in general. Just those three things! Nothing more.

Be the best

We owe it to ourselves to be as good as we possibly can and we can be good if we take the time to digest and employ SSF. We can send our audience home saying, 'Wow! That was good!' Being in that positive mental state to bring SSF together and get it working for us will have the desired effect. There is nothing quite as empowering as knowing that you have a good game and are a match for anyone in your own inimitable way. When you embrace The Clinton Factor you will improve your performance in every area of your life. Do it now!

Just a few things to remember with regard to your mental status:

• If you are ever feeling anxious before a presentation or a speaking performance of any kind – remember to use the five-point programme in this chapter to help reduce your state of anxiety.

- Before you have any form of communication, remember the inseparable link between mental and emotional status and check exactly how you are feeling. Are you in the right frame of mind to engage in this piece of communication or are you likely to have a negative effect on the person or people you are about to connect with?

Use any of the exercises in the vocal or physical status sections to help create the right frame of mind, especially the breathing exercises. They will also help to relieve anxiety.

16

status in business

It is absolutely vital that we recognize and adopt the right status for our business lives. On The Clinton Factor scale of 1 to 10 it is 5 to 7 every time.

If we are going to function with maximum effect in our working lives we need to have that open and neutral status that lets others in. If we close ourselves down with a status that is too low or too high then we'll be denying those we do business with access to ourselves thus making any meaningful communication impossible. So many people make the mistake of adopting a level of status that they believe is in line with their position. In fact, for some, it is the excuse they have been looking for to 'lord it' over their subordinates. Wrong! As we said earlier the kind of status we are talking about in this book has nothing to do with position or hierarchy, it is about how we are perceived regardless of title or position in the pecking order.

Be afraid – be very afraid!

We must stay on the look out for anyone who uses their position to flex their muscles and assume their status is higher than those around them. If we look at the aggressively high status man in Chapter 12 we will find a person whose status actually gets in the way of productive work. He believes that he will get the best out of people by shouting at them and keeping them in a constant state of fear. What a fool! The reverse is actually true. Those working under this person will be more prone to make mistakes and will then try to cover up their errors and sweep them under the carpet. It will only be a matter of time before King Kong looks underneath the carpet and explodes. This person may well be very clever and have a great knowledge of his subject but by using the wrong level of status his people skills will be zero and his department's productivity nil.

What's your handicap?

We once worked with a man who would boast about the dressing downs he dished out to his workforce and firmly believed that these tongue-lashings were having a positive effect. He also enjoyed telling stories about putting people down and scoring points over those around him. He was a keen golfer and one of these stories was about a member of his staff who tried to curry favour by suggesting they had a round of golf together. This is how our man responded:

'Look, Ken – you play off 24, I play off six – you're going to lose a lot of balls and I'm not. You're going to feel bad when you're in the trees trying to get on the fairway and I'm going to get frustrated with you. I do not want a six-hour round of golf thank you. Maybe in a couple of year's time when you've stopped hacking round. Okay.'

He told this story almost as if he was being cruel to be kind but the subtext was how good he was at putting people in their place. Not only was the level of status wrong, he could not see that he had missed a golden opportunity. A boss with the right level of status and the right understanding of the needs of his staff would have accepted the invitation and looked on a quick nine holes as a way of getting to know the man better and even helping him with some useful tips about his swing.

What was his handicap? His inability to communicate properly.

The third man

One of our colleagues came up with an interesting theory about people who play high status. She was working with a senior business figure from a major UK company who could never be wrong. This man was usually late for a session but was never able to apologize. On one occasion when arriving 30 minutes late he spoke about himself in the third person and rather grandly announced: 'He's arrived!'

Extraordinary behaviour! Her observation and conclusion as to why this man behaved in that way was that high status people can be afraid that they won't be liked if they reveal themselves. This, of course, demonstrates a fundamental weakness. When dealing with high status people in our business lives we must always remember this: claiming status over others will make us look insecure. People who wish to establish a higher status than others will never be at an advantage. We must never assume that our status is higher than others. We must never assume that we are better or worse than others. We must always recognize the worth of others without backing down or fronting up and only a middle level of status can achieve this – the Clinton level.

They all hate me!

Dangerous levels of high status are always the most apparent in a business environment. People often make the huge mistake of associating success with high status. They couldn't be more wrong. Yes, some people achieve success in their business lives by adopting unreasonably high levels of status and thus incur low levels of popularity. They most likely won't even be aware of or, quite possibly, even care about their unpopularity. When a person succeeds in making themselves unpopular they have failed. They have made a bad choice. They have poisoned the atmosphere and are unlikely to get the best out of colleagues – both junior and, surprisingly, senior. By opting for the middle ground they might have been even more successful and certainly more popular. What is the point of saying, 'Look at what I have achieved!' if nobody likes you? There are, of course, those who get a perverse kind of pleasure out of not being liked because they believe that if they are feared that will give them power. We think that's a rather twisted outlook. Great communicators do not rule by fear. Great communicators manage their businesses successfully because they have learned to listen, they have learned to be aware, they have learned to understand the views and values of those around them and they have only been able to do this by assuming the right level of status. The extremes are as bad as each other – only the middle ground will do.

The interview

When attending job interviews we have all had bad experiences at the hands of our interviewers because of their appalling choice of status. Let's look at three different scenarios of being greeted for the first time.

1 The interviewer remains behind their desk, half rises to shake hands, just about manages to look at you though their eyebrows and mumbles some sort of greeting.

2 The interviewer remains seated behind their desk, orders you to take a seat and gestures towards the chair opposite without looking up.

3 The interviewer comes out of their room to collect you, shakes you warmly by the hand, introduces themselves and asks how your journey was.

In the first case, by demonstrating low status characteristics, the interviewer has virtually shut down any meaningful communication and has probably stopped you from having any respect for them. In the second case, through high status behaviour, the interviewer has closed off proper communication and has probably either intimidated you or just annoyed you. The third interviewer has done everything right by going for the middle ground and has brought about the right conditions for good communication. It's not difficult and the benefits are great. The first two interviewers immediately threw up barriers that were going to be difficult, if not impossible, to overcome. What madness! The third interviewer seemed pleased to meet you and by greeting you outside of the room put you at ease in their environment. They then showed an interest in your journey (i.e. you) by striking up a cordial conversation and again putting you at ease. What they did was to create a situation where they are going to get the very best out of you and not miss the opportunity that you could be great for their company. Again 5 to 7 every time. It's a no-brainer!

Who will buy?

Let's look at another business situation: sales. Never was there a more important area for getting the level of status absolutely bang on. If we do not use the right level of status in sales we stand little or no chance of ever selling anything. There might be a remote possibility that the low status salesperson will get an order because the buyer feels sorry for them but that will be a one-off. There could be a slim chance that a high status salesperson might make a sale through intimidation but repeat business is unlikely. No, the best way to succeed in sales is through The Clinton Factor of status – 5 to 7 – open, accessible, warm and non-threatening.

Sales is not about selling. Anyone who thinks that they are going to go out there and sell to people is barking up the wrong tree. People do not like being sold to. Successful sales can only be achieved by building relationships and that is not achievable for low and high status people. Low and high status salespeople are not capable of forging long-term, meaningful relationships with clients. A client has to feel that they can trust a salesperson. A client must not feel that they are having something pushed at them that they neither want nor need. Only an open and neutral status can be successful in sales. Buyers need to operate in the comfort of a situation in which they are not going to be hit by the hard sell. They want to be in a situation where their supplier is a friend and adviser not someone who wants to fill up the order book as quickly as possible. The lower status salesperson is unlikely to operate the hard sell but the high status salesperson may well do so. Middle ground status in sales is where business can flourish with no one feeling pressured to buy or make a sale. It's so simple and it works! People in sales generally tend to be in the middle to high level of status bracket but it is the middle level that will be more successful. Anyone who adopts The Clinton Factor level of status in their life in sales will enjoy long-lasting and fruitful relationships with their clients.

The relationship

Successful middle ground status in sales is about being there for your clients at all times – not just when you want an order or a contract. It's a little bit like Bill after 9/11. We spoke in the first chapter of Bill being open, warm, accessible and strong for the people who needed that. Being there for our clients regardless of financial gain is very similar. It's about giving, not taking. Middle status people are givers and it's givers who get. Low and high status take. They can bleed a person dry emotionally and that's no way to operate in business. It is the low key offering of help, guidance and expertise that will always pay dividends. If you want something from somebody, be prepared to give something of yourself.

Bill Clinton always appears to be giving and sharing. Only a middle ground neutral status can do that. That is where we need to be in order to have a positive impact in our business lives.

The one-day experiment

This is something we should all do on a regular basis. The next time you go into work analyse every single piece of communication you have. Think very carefully about how you address and interact with everyone you come into contact with from the caretaker to the chairman of the board.

- Did you acknowledge the person who runs the car park?
- Did you say good morning to the person who sold you your train ticket?
- Did you say hello to the person on reception or did you walk straight past?
- Did you ask your PA about their weekend?
- Did you speak to the person at the next desk or in the next office and find out how they are?
- Did you make a list of who you need to contact today?
- Did you make a list of who you don't need to contact but it might be good if you could?
- Did you ask the person who serves you your lunch how they are?
- Did you think about each piece of communication beforehand to make sure that you approached it in a positive way?

It really doesn't take a lot to do any of this but the benefits could be huge and the good feeling that you create will spread through the building. Imagine what might happen if everyone did the one-day experiment – a happy working environment. Imagine what might happen if everyone did the one-day experiment every day – the company's productivity would almost certainly increase. It's 5 to 7 every time.

17

status on stage

> *'Acting is all about honesty. If you can fake that you've got it made.'*
>
> George Burns (attrib.)

Status on stage is a bit like status in life. Acting is, after all, art reflecting life. Status on stage has a very broad spectrum. Understanding the extremes of status is very important when finding The Clinton Factor level of status. Theatre is probably the finest medium to demonstrate the extremes of status.

It is an actor's job to explore status and to keep an eye out for its subtle changes and react accordingly. During their careers actors will have discovered and hopefully played every level of status to be found in the theatre. This is what makes the job of the actor fascinating. If an actor is unaware of status and its varying degrees then they will not succeed in their work. The success of every piece of theatre is dependent on the fluctuation of the status of the characters in the play. Every time a new character appears on stage the status of the characters already in the space should shift, if only slightly, to accommodate the new person on stage. If this does not happen then there is something wrong with the production.

Is it working?

Examining status on stage is a wonderful way of gauging if a production is on the right track. Actors, directors and writers are all well advised to pay special attention to where the status of their characters is at every point in the play. If something doesn't feel right, look right, sound right, or if the play just isn't working for some reason, check the status of the characters and if they are being correctly affected by the other characters in the piece. This usually sorts things out!

The shifting plates of theatre

The most powerful and dramatic pieces of theatre are when massive shifts of status occur, for example, when kings are deposed or when even stranger things are at play, as in the case of Richard II who deliberately reduced his status to martyrdom by his abdication. There are wonderful swinging changes of status throughout Shakespeare's *Julius Caesar*. A man's status is reduced to nothing when a powerful nobleman is wrongfully incarcerated, as in *The Count of Monte Cristo* who creates yet another massive status shift on his return to society. Great examples of ever-shifting status can be found in more contemporary pieces of theatre such as Noel Coward's *Hay Fever* or *The Sea* by Edward Bond. It is when such great changes of status happen that an audience gasps and we know that the play is working well.

It is useful for us to remember and remind ourselves about these dramatic changes of status on stage. When we observe the pendulum of status it becomes absolutely apparent how damaging the extremes can be. We may feel that the damage we see in the theatre has no bearing on our own lives in the real world but we'd be wrong. We will all, at some stage, be subject to someone using extremes of status for their own gain and this will be, at the least, unpleasant. This pratice can be manipulative and used for self-preservation at the expense of others. It might also reflect a lack of self-confidence, which is highly evident in the blustering bully. The more we understand about status and its extremes, and the more we are aware of it, the less damage we will suffer.

The more soundly based we are in our own middle status, the better equipped we will be to counteract the assault of extreme status. Abusers of extreme status in plays invariably get their comeuppance – the same is largely true in life. If we think about the abusive despots throughout history, it is reasonably true to say that they have almost all met a sticky end. If you take high status it is there to be taken away. If you adopt manipulative low status you will eventually be rumbled. No one can reasonably take exception to an open and neutral status.

Once more unto the breach

One of the best examples of the success of mid-level status on stage is in Shakespeare's *Henry V*. If you do not have time to read the play or to experience it in a theatre, go online to Youtube and take a look at Henry V's Saint Crispin's Day speech as performed by both Lawrence Olivier and Kenneth Branagh. The same words delivered in completely different ways but with the same level of status. The story is that Henry's army, which is made up of the soldiers of noblemen loyal to him, are battle weary and vastly outnumbered when they encounter the might of the French army at Agincourt. The speech takes place minutes before both armies engage each other in combat. It is a heartfelt motivational speech of thanks that inspires the English soldiers to victory. The adoption of mid-level status in both performances is so moving that many would wish themselves there to take up arms. Historians will tell us that the noblemen of England who fought that day did not follow Henry because he ordered them to (in fact Henry had to humbly ask for their help) nor did they take part because they felt sorry for him. They were there for him because of his great leadership through mid-level status.

The next time you are in the theatre, pay special attention to the status levels of the characters and see how they change and develop throughout the play. If there is no shift of status when a new character enters, then you are watching a poor piece of theatre. If there is a constant fluctuation of status levels in the piece, the director and the actors are doing their jobs properly. The actors will be 'mirroring life'. They may be doing this in a somewhat dramatic way – but they are, nevertheless, reflecting reality by their fine observation of character status. When you next visit the cinema do the same. A good piece of filmmaking will have the necessary shifts of status. If it does not it is an inferior production. Actors on screen will use status in the same way that actors on stage do. It may be done a little more subtly, a flick of the eye, a slight adjustment of posture or a tiny change of voice pitch. The only difference between the shifts of status in theatre and life is that the former may be heightened for dramatic effect – otherwise they are exactly the same.

Observing status levels and their effects on stage and film is a great way of identifying and understanding how status works and it's safer than doing it in public and running the risk of upsetting someone in real life by staring at them.

'I love acting. It is so much more real than life.'

Oscar Wilde

Bill on the boards

We should now talk about Bill Clinton's status on stage. It is one of total accessibility. Not only accessible but giving the audience a feeling of actually being drawn in. Perfectly pitched middle ground status – open, warm, committed and strong. No fluctuation. Confident in that 5 to 7 area. Veering towards 7 when points need to be made and reinforced. Hovering around 5 when heartfelt statements are delivered. Never outside 5 to 7. No apologies. No finger jabbing rhetoric. Nothing that could be considered remotely offensive. Every word delivered with authority and conviction without being dogmatic or dictatorial.

Clinton's public addresses as Governor and President were consistently on the 7 side of the 5 to 7 bracket, anything higher would have taken him away from the very people he was trying to reach. Even when on stage as a former President, Clinton maintains the same level of status he did throughout his various roles in office. This level of status seems to filter through all areas of Clinton's public life and the consistency gives a comfort and a surety to those he comes into contact with. It is pretty much failsafe – it certainly works for him and it can work for you.

18

status in life

'Happiness is when what you think, what you say and what you do are in harmony.'

Mahatma Gandhi

It may seem a little corny but Gandhi got it right. Bringing all the aspects of mid-level status together is the perfect recipe for achieving the very best we can in every area of our lives. It may take a little effort but the rewards will be great. We have seen what can be done with mid-level status in our business lives and when performing – now we need to apply the same principles to our lives in general.

By now there should be absolutely no argument that the 5 to 7 channel is where we need to be – the area where The Clinton Factor is most effective. Let's think back to that rather idealistic notion we spoke about earlier in this book where everyone woke up one morning with mid-level status and what a wonderful world that would create. Okay, it's not going to happen in a global sense, but we can make it happen in our own worlds. We can have a positive effect on those around us and see how great the ripple effect might be. There can be no doubt that other people will feel the benefit of our mid-level status and that, in turn, will make us feel good too. A circle of positive feedback!

'It's very hard to be happy if you're not good and it's very easy to be good if you're happy.'

Steven Fry

We can all have that marvellously empowering feeling that mid-level status brings. That confidence in the knowledge that we have equipped ourselves to deal with any difficult situations with our strength in mid-level status. The happiness we can get from getting the best out of the important people in our personal and business lives. The satisfaction we can achieve by creating win–win situations.

Essentially this book has been written to help people improve their performances when standing and speaking but why not take The Clinton Factor a little further? Why not apply it to everything we do? Mid-level status is, after all, the bedrock of every piece of communication we are involved with. If this book can help with life in general we will be all be very happy people. Give it a go!

The Clinton Factor is for life!

19

star status

Star status is something we would all like to have but what is it? Astronomy aside, what is a star? What type of person are we referring to? Film star, rock star, pop star, star in sport, star in industry, star of the political arena – what is this star thing? It probably means different things to different people. That certain *je ne sais quoi*, the little bit extra, the X factor. Money, fame, talent, notoriety, intellect can all play a part in star quality. 'Oh she's such a star!' can mean a number of things – a great singer, actor, businessperson. 'My boss is such a star' usually means that they let you go home early or do something else that makes you happy. 'Star quality', where status is concerned, is about charisma.

Communicating with charisma

The Clinton Factor is all about communicating with charisma – so what is charisma? Here we go again! Well, we need to know or at least have an idea about what it may mean. Once again it will mean different things to different people. One person's charismatic leader will not be another's. The *Concise Oxford English Dictionary* describes it thus:

> **Charisma** *n* (*pl.* charismata) **1a** the ability to inspire followers with devotion and enthusiasm. **b** an attractive aura; great charm. **2** a divinely conferred power or talent. [ecclesiastical Latin from Greek *kharisma*, from *kharis*' favour, grace]

Any wiser? Possibly not, which is why we all have our own meaning for charisma. Essentially it has to be a quality or qualities that draw people to certain other people. However we describe it, it's a very powerful force. It's a personal power and personal power will always be stronger than positional power. It's about being liked and/or respected. To be liked and respected it helps if we have self-belief, confidence and enthusiasm for the things we do. These are positive qualities that make us attractive to others and they must be communicated.

The leader

We said that personal power is stronger than positional power which is, of course, true, but personal power is key for those who wish to obtain positional power. The great leaders throughout history have all possessed immense personal power or charisma. Churchill, Roosevelt, Ghandi, Mandela, Kennedy, Clinton – every one of them equipped with the skills of inspiring and motivating. These people are not unique in their qualities; they have simply recognized their skills and used them to communicate their vision to others. In return those around them bring creativity and commitment to their work. They feel empowered by their leader's confidence in them and are gratified by their approval. The charismatic qualities of these leaders draw people around them into an emotional bond. They feel valued and worthy. They are infected with their leader's zest and passion, and are happy to do their bidding. This is the power of the charismatic leader, one who is an indomitable force that fires the imagination and intelligence of all those around. They build trust and make dreams tangible. They use their energy to generate excitement and enthusiasm. They are people who have changed the course of history through their personalities.

Have you got it?

Yes you have! We all have to varying degrees and we can all improve our personal charisma. We can all be more appealing than we already are and it's largely about status. Genuine mid-level status is the way to go. Low status will not command respect – high status will have an initial shock impact but will ultimately close us down. Charismatic people appear open and strong and genuine mid-level status will provide an undeniable strength that we find appealing.

Keep in shape

We don't have to go to the gym to create the kind of physical status that's going to enhance our charisma. Remember that it's all about being accessible. By avoiding the extremes of low and high physical status we will allow people access to us. Low physical status will close us off and high physical status will push people away. Mid-level physical status helps to build an aura that people are not only comfortable with but actually feel drawn to.

It must be said

Speaking is crucial to charisma. Language and delivery are vital means to influence and persuasion. Engaging in dialogue with our audiences – even an audience of one – is how we make our charisma work for us: presenting and stimulating others with our ideas and enlisting their help. We must, therefore, pay particular attention to our vocal status. We represent ourselves with our words and the pitch and tone with which they are delivered. Our voice is the most important and most powerful instrument we possess. We do not want to apologize for ourselves vocally nor do we wish to appear pompous and arrogant. Once again it is that mid-level vocal status that will serve as the platform for positive and effective communication.

Stay in tune

If we do not have empathy with those we come into contact with our charisma rating will plummet. It doesn't take a lot to gain a person's appreciation. It's that listening thing again. Taking an interest. Enjoying someone else's success. Creating feelings of equality and relating to people on their level. Being attuned to the emotions of others is one of the major keys to successful communication. It makes people feel that they can work with us, trust us and even confide in us. When bonds are created in an empathic atmosphere they are easy to maintain and can last a lifetime. Stay in tune.

Superstar

It would be great to think that we are liked and respected and that we can improve our appeal to others. Well, we can do this simply by keeping a constant check on our levels of status. If we do, we will be more charismatic and communicating will become easier and more effective. We will be communicating with charisma. The vast majority of us may never aspire to the dizzy heights to which some people's charisma has taken them. We may not achieve 'star status' but we can certainly be 'superstars' in our own right – in our own sphere of influence – and that has to be appealing.

The man in question

There can be little argument that Bill Clinton has great personal power or charisma which undoubtedly comes from his open and accessible levels of status. When we decided to write a book about communication skills, we thought it would be helpful to have public figure in mind who had what we believed to be 'star status' and, politics aside, Bill seemed to fill this role quite naturally. We must never underestimate the power of mid-level status. Clinton is an example of mid-level status as a potent force, of what can be achieved by avoiding the extremes. At the risk of banging on – it's 5 to 7 every time – the Clinton channel.

part
four

focus

In this part you will learn:
- to understand the power of the three circles of concentration
- how to distribute your focus amongst your audience
- how to manage the focus of your audience.

20

what is focus?

We all understand the importance of being focused but what does it actually mean and how can it improve our performance? Focus and concentration are major contributors to our success in life – domestic, social or business. If we do not focus and concentrate on the things that are important to us we are sure to fail. Whether we are studying for an exam, working on a report or creating a presentation, focus and concentration are paramount. They are particularly important when we are 'performing'. We must be focused from the moment we enter the performance area to the moment we leave it. If we are not we will lose our audience and stand little or no chance of managing their focus. Once we have decided what we are going to say and have adopted the right status for the job, it is time to apply focus to our delivery.

Enjoying the show Mrs Lincoln?

Watching the best actors deliver their lines is an object lesson in the effective management of focus. Whether it is on stage or on film the skill of successfully directing focus is a prerequisite for all actors – without it their performances will count for nothing. When we watch a good piece of theatre or film our focus and attention will move seamlessly between the characters on stage – this is because the actors are doing their jobs properly. With their own focus and concentration, they are steering our attention to where it needs to be for the piece to make sense. If an actor is only concerned with their own performance and not the piece as a whole they will pull focus and divert our attention from where it should be. Some actors pull focus by visibly reacting to everything that is said without actually listening – these people shouldn't be allowed near a stage or a camera.

> *'Chuck it to them, and say to yourself if it's their scene not mine. But if it really is your scene – grab it!'*
>
> John Hurt

The focus puller

In the film industry the focus puller has the extremely important job of managing the focus of the camera and measuring the shot. In life the focus puller has a very negative connotation. They will always 'grab it' whether it is theirs to grab or not, and we all know who they are. They appear in every walk of life.

They are at work, they are probably in your family and even among the people you socialize with. They will dominate; they care little or nothing for others. They are attention seekers who will do anything to snatch the focus in any situation ('me me me me...'). Get rid of them!

Now's the time

Actors must live in the 'now'. It is essential that all performers are performing in the present and not getting ahead of themselves. They need to know their material so well that they do not have to think ahead and can focus on the now. This is often a problem with focus pullers who have already decided how they are going to react (whether it is necessary to do so or not) and get ahead of themselves and telegraph what's coming. Atrocious!

It's not just bad actors that get ahead of themselves. A great many people who have to stand and deliver are guilty of not living in the now when they perform and this is not because they are self-centred like the hams on stage: it can be for a number of non-egocentric reasons. It might be because they have a very quick mind and they are already thinking ahead to the next page of their presentation rather than staying with the moment. It may be because they would rather be anywhere else and that the sooner they finish the better they will feel. Either way they are doing themselves a great disservice and are short-changing their audience.

We need to stop and think what we are doing. Racing through a presentation will destroy the focus of an audience and it will not make us feel any better. We must deliver three times more slowly than we would read in our head. Living and performing in the now will hold an audience's attention and give the speaker more satisfaction as a result. Let's start living in the now.

Easy does it

When we are being trained in presentation or public speaking skills we will almost always be told to slow down but we also need to understand why we are galloping through our material and with that understanding focus on the needs of our audience. When we have done that and are performing in the now we will have taken an enormous step towards improving our delivery and pleasing our audience. It's very easy to understand the logic behind being in the now but it is perhaps even easier to drift back into giving a breakneck paced delivery. Let's live and focus in the now!

Focus on Bill

Bill Clinton is a grand master when it comes to focus. Every moment for Bill is a 'now' moment. What is most important to Bill is what he is saying at that particular moment and the effect it is having on those who are listening to him at that moment. What is important to Bill is that he has the full attention of his audience and that he has not lost them by racing ahead even though he has an extremely quick brain. Bill Clinton clearly understands the power of focus and uses it with tremendous effect.

Pacino, de Niro, Clinton

Actors sometimes make very good politicians but could it just as easily happen the other way round – or has it? Not sure about that. When we watch Bill Clinton perform there is a more than a hint that there is a very good actor waiting to leap out. His mastery of focus certainly equips him to play many roles well. So maybe it could happen the other way round. We will probably never know. One thing we do know is that Clinton did once consider a career in music so his talent and desire of the performing arts is very apparent. He was also an admirer of Ronald Reagan as a communicator – someone who changed careers the other way round. Anything is possible. Time will tell.

What do we need to do?

So, let's assume that we are starting to pay greater attention to the importance of focus and concentration. How do we build on that? How do we enhance our performance with the power of focus? Well, in the way that actors are able to guide the focus of their audience around the stage in order for them to follow the story, presenting in public is much the same. The only big difference is the abolition of the 'fourth wall'. The fourth wall in theatre is the invisible wall that separates the audience from the stage. Only when performing in pantomime or delivering asides in restoration comedy or melodrama will an actor speak directly to an audience. A presenter speaks directly to an audience all the time. Rather than steering an audience's focus through the story of a play, the speaker has to use focus to guide their audience through the story of their presentation or speech. If you agreed with what we said at the beginning of this book you will know that every piece of communication is, in fact, a story.

Stan's the man

When actors train they will almost certainly study the teachings of Konstantin Stanislavski, the man who created the first 'system' of acting. Stanislavski paid particular attention to focus and concentration. He believed that an audience's focus could be managed by using the three circles of concentration or circles of attention. Let's call them the circles of concentration.

There are many different styles of presenting and there is no hard and fast rule as to which is right. There is, however, one method that really does need to be avoided. We have all witnessed the speaker that buries their face in their notes. The speaker who does not look up from their notes. The speaker who is simply reading to us. This kind of presentation does not really connect with an audience. If we are just going to look down and read what is on the paper we will not be able to use the circles of concentration and we will definitely not be able to manage the focus of our audience. It is possible to use both notes and the circles but the speaker must be able to lift the message off the page and deliver it out front.

Konstantin Stanislavski (1863–1938)

Stanislavski was born Konstantin Sergeyevich Alekseyev in Moscow in the time of Czarist Russia and Peter the Great. His father was a wealthy merchant who had made the family fortune through the manufacture of gold and silver thread.

Interested in theatre from an early age Konstantin took the stage name Stanislavski at the age of 25 and set up the Moscow Society of Art and Literature. In 1898 he co-founded the Moscow Art Theatre, the first ensemble theatre in Russia.

At the Moscow Art Theatre, Stanislavski started to develop his own system of training actors, which would help them achieve a more realistic and believable style of acting. He challenged the traditional ideas of the day about drama and performance and pioneered a more naturalist school of thought. He used his system to succeed, like no other director or producer, in bringing the works of playwrights like Chekov and Gorki to life.

Chekhov and Stanislavski's collaboration at Moscow Art Theatre resulted in the creation of the stage classics *The Seagull*, *Uncle Vanya*, *The Three Sisters*, and *The Cherry Orchard*. Stanislavski also starred in several classical plays as an actor himself. His performances as Othello and as Gayev in Chekhov's *The Cherry Orchard* were highly acclaimed by critics and the public alike.

His process of character development, the 'Stanislavski Method', was the catalyst for the development of method acting. Method acting, or 'The Method' as it is known, is said by many to be the most influential acting system ever developed. It was first popularized by the Group Theatre in New York in the 1930s and then advanced by Lee Strasberg at The Actors' Studio in the 1940s and 1950s. The Actors' Studio is still running today as a non-profit organization for professional actors, directors and playwrights. It has its headquarters in New York with a branch in West Hollywood. At the time of going to print, Ellen Burtsyn, Harvey Keitel and Al Pacino were co-presidents.

The Stanislavski system is still the basis for a large part of our actor training and practice. His methods and theories are still read today in his books, including *My Life in Art* (1924), *An Actor Prepares* (1926), and *Building a Character* (1950). His house in central Moscow is now a public museum dedicated to his life.

Stanislavski wanted to find an approach to acting that would be of benefit to all actors but he himself famously said of his own system: 'Create your own method. Don't depend slavishly on mine. Make up something that will work for you. But keep breaking traditions I beg you.'

The godfather of method acting

How does an actor act? That was the question Stanislavski dedicated his life to exploring. His work proved to be an enormous contribution to 20th century theatre and film, and his legacy lives on today.

Many actors have been influenced by Stanislavski and some directors would say that Stanislavski has had an influence on every good actor in the world.

Stanislavski quotes

'The program for our undertaking was revolutionary. We protested against the old manner of acting and against theatricality, against artificial pathos and declamation...'

'What is important to me is not the truth outside myself, but the truth within myself.'

'At times of great stress it is especially necessary to achieve a complete freeing of the muscles.'

'Remember: there are no small parts, only small actors.'

'When we are on stage, we are in the here and now.'

'All action on the stage must have an inner justification, be logical, coherent, and real.'

'When an actor is completely absorbed by some profoundly moving objective so that he throws his whole being passionately into its execution, he reaches a state we call inspiration.'

'Bring yourself to the part of taking hold of a role, as if it were your own life. Speak for your character in your own person. When you sense this real kinship to your part, your newly created being will become soul of your soul, flesh of your flesh.'

'The actor must believe in everything that takes place on the stage – and most of all – in what he himself is doing – and one can only believe in the truth.'

'If you know your character's thoughts, the proper vocal and bodily expressions will naturally follow.'

21

the world is a circle

'It usually takes more than three weeks to prepare a good impromptu speech.'

Mark Twain

You will, no doubt, have been told that there is no substitute for good preparation. This is, of course, true and if we are to move to a higher level of performance then good preparation and familiarization is essential.

Let's assume that we have done our homework and prepared well. We have washed down the walls, we have sanded the woodwork and put on the undercoat, rolled on the emulsion – time now to to apply the gloss. We have a good story that is constructed well, that travels with fluidity, that is brutally edited yet is alive with spontaneity. We have adopted the perfect middle ground status that makes us strong and accessible. Time to bring the circles into play!

What's in a circle?

We like to describe the three circles of concentration in filmic terms:

- third circle – the master shot;
- second circle – the intimate two shot;
- first circle – the single close up.

'What on earth does that mean?' we hear you scream! Let's break things down.

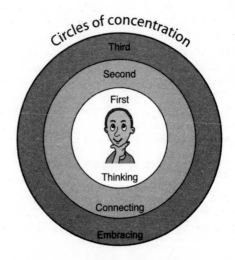

Third circle

This is the establishing or master shot. The shot that sets the scene. Imagine you are a film director. There you are sitting in your wood and canvas chair with your name on the back looking like Steven Spielberg. The clapper board reveals the name of the movie, *Focus – this time it's personal!* The first thing you need to do is to create a platform to work from – a solid base. One shot that could, if necessary, tell the story of the scene. This is what is known in the business as the master shot – the safety shot. It's a shot that can be cut back to in order to re-establish where we are in the plot. It's our failsafe. There is little or no point in progressing any further with our movie until we are happy with our master shot – it is the very foundation and without that continuity we do not have a film.

How does this relate to our presentations and speeches? Well, in much the same way as a film maker requires a platform to work from so do speakers. We need our own master shot – our safety shot that we can return to when we need to establish our relationship with our audience. The only difference being that as speakers we never leave our third circle of concentration. We are constantly in third. From our third circle of concentration we are able to engage second and first which will we come to later. We will be able to cut into our master shot to create our own 'presentation movie'.

The energy of the third circle

Our third circle is the energy with which we engage our audience. We need to be able think a little abstractly here. We all generate an energy when we stand up to speak – some more than others. This is something that we need to be very aware as it's something that we can control. This is an energy that most of us will need to increase. This energy takes in our whole audience – it embraces everyone in the working space and we must maintain the optimum level of third circle energy at all times. When we have acquired a high level of third circle energy we will be well on the way to completing The Clinton Factor puzzle.

Use the force

A few months ago we were invited by a client, the world's leading interactive services provider, to join them for an event at the O_2 Arena in London where Bill Clinton was speaking.

Meeting the former President was no disappointment – this is a man who does exactly what it says on the tin! Without wishing to sound sycophantic, when Bill Clinton entered the room it was as if someone had flipped the on switch to a whole new bank of lights – a new and effective energy had entered the room. This was a man who had no problem inhabiting that third circle of concentration and maintaining its energy. Later when he was introduced on stage to speak it was abundantly clear that he was still very much in that third circle. He calmly entered on stage, took in the audience with a smile as he approached the podium, carefully arranged his notes, slowly removed his glasses case from his inside pocket, equally slowly removed his glasses from the case and put them on, looked up and engaged his audience once again. This process probably took around about a minute and at no time were we allowed to escape the Clinton third circle of concentration. He had us!

What is this energy force thing? This third circle stuff probably sounds a bit weird. Maybe it is a bit weird, but what we have to do is connect with those on the perimeter of our audience. In a conventional theatre style presentation we must consciously think about including the people on the sides of the auditorium and those at the very back which can sometimes call for a bigger performance than we might be comfortable with. Don't worry – it may feel a little strange or even over the top but it will not appear like that to our audience, in fact they will think more of us for including everyone in our address and not just those in the first few rows.

Here's another little abstract thought to wrestle with – by sending out our energy of third circle to the outer reaches of our audience, our energy and attention will automatically fall on those people inside the perimeter of our audience – nobody will feel left out. Third circle energy neglects no one. Third circle is the focus starting point for any form of public address. When in doubt include everyone. Get the message to the back and the sides – if we do that then those in the middle will automatically be taken care of. It's the safety shot. Presentational skills trainers will always tell you that you must project your voice to the back of the space so everyone can hear you. Well, yes, but you could look down at the floor and be heard at the back – so it's a little bit more than that and that is why we talk about energy. Physical, vocal and emotional energy are needed in equal quantities to sustain third circle focus. And remember, we never leave our third circle of concentration. Hopefully third circle is starting to feel a little less weird. Third circle – it's our focus base.

When story and status are working well we can use focus to colour our performance and third circle is the foundation of that focus. What Bill Clinton did with his third circle of concentration at the O₂ Arena we are all capable of doing. Once we acknowledge the effect that third circle energy can have on an audience we can work to apply it. When presenting to a large audience third circle is probably the most important of the three. In fact when working in a large space one can almost scrape by without using second and first if necessary.

The next time you are at the theatre pay special attention to see if the actors are using their third circle with good effect. If you are watching a quality piece of theatre the actors will certainly be maximizing the impact of their third circle of concentration to connect with the audience. They may not be addressing the audience directly but they will be using their third circle energy to engage them.

When the focus base of third circle is working well, a good presenter can slip in and out of second and first whilst remaining in third to give a variety of focus. This is where the circles of concentration come into their own. This is where a speaker who has embraced the value of the circles can switch, steer and hold an audience's focus. If a speaker loses focus, their audience will cease to be engaged and entertained. So how do we move from pure third to second circle?

Second circle

This is the intimate two shot. While we might call it the intimate two shot we are, of course, concentrating on the focus of one person – the speaker – who in turn will distribute their own focus between individuals or groups of people.

The window to the soul

Anyone who has had any form of presentation skills training will have been told, 'You've got to have eye contact you know.' Well, yes this is true but what does it mean? And why? And how long for? We'll deal with these questions in a moment but first, why is eye contact so important? It's important because it means that we are connecting with people. We are paying attention to others. We are showing an interest in those around us and that doesn't just mean the people we are addressing in a presentation. It's important that we have eye contact with those we are engaging with no matter what the situation. Whether we are having a casual conversation at work, whether we are being introduced to someone new, or whether we are giving a report to the boss we have to look them in the eye – it shows respect. It also helps us to gauge their reaction to what we are saying and allows them to do the same.

> *'Find your mark, look the other fellow in the eye and tell the truth.'*
>
> James Cagney

It's all very well being told that we must have eye contact with our audience but what if we are addressing over a hundred people? Can we possibly have eye contact with everyone? Of course not, but through our random selection of those we do make eye contact with we can give the impression that we are personally addressing everyone. This is something that Clinton does brilliantly well. Even when he is using an autocue the personal touch is still there. With George W. Bush on the other hand it is quite obvious that he is using an autocue. He will start with the two on the right, progress to the one in the middle and then the two on the left and back again in a ridiculous, robotic 'lighthouse sweep'. Clinton's use of the autocue is so random you wouldn't know it was there at all. Comparing the two we see a colossal difference in performance technique through focus management. One is infinitely more watchable than the other.

Still lookin'?

> *'You lookin' at me?'*
>
> Robert de Niro (in *Taxi Driver*)

How long for?

In a one-to-one conversation we might hold eye contact all the way through – it's a matter of being sensitive to how the other person feels about it. When addressing an audience it's three to four seconds tops! If we look at one person out of an audience of 200 people for too long that person is going to feel very uncomfortable and the other 199 will feel ignored and left out. It is important to shift our second circle of concentration frequently. This is what Clinton does and that is what makes his audiences feel personally addressed even though he hasn't managed to take them all in individually.

In the limelight

TV news readers and presenters have a natural choice of focus with second circle and they engage with us almost entirely through that circle alone – even though they are subconsciously still in third.

Actors can use second circle of concentration with great dramatic effect. As John Hurt indicated in his quote we used in the previous chapter – second circle is a wonderful tool to centre the focus on other people and it can also be used to reverse that focus back on to ourselves. Let's take a look at some classic examples of great second circle of concentration from the movies.

Absent fish

It is probably safe to say that everyone has seen *Jaws*. There is a marvellous scene midway through the film where Robert Shaw, Richard Dreyfuss and Roy Scheider are at sea at night drinking below deck. Shaw tells the story of his ship being torpedoed in the South Atlantic during the war. The men were helpless in the icy water and were slowly being picked off by the sharks. During this story Shaw ignores Dreyfuss and focuses on Scheider. The story he tells is rather harrowing and lasts for about two minutes. During that period Shaw never takes his eyes off Scheider – he doesn't even appear to blink. This choice of heightened second circle of concentration makes the story especially chilling. His tone is measured, the volume low and the intensity of his focus makes this scene one of the most powerful in the film – without a fish in sight.

You may think so – I couldn't possibly comment

You may remember a wonderful BBC series called *The House of Cards* with Ian Richardson playing Sir Francis Urquhart, Chief Whip turned Prime Minister. Writer Andrew Davies used the old restoration style aside to great effect in a modern day context. We all waited with anticipation for the next time when Richardson would use the device to step outside of the action, fix us with his steely blue eyes and deliver a 'little do they know' style quip.

What's my name?

In *Gladiator*, Russell Crowe does a fine job with second circle when he addresses the man who killed his family. Crowe looks the actor firmly in the eye and tells him who he is. In the same way as Shaw's story in *Jaws,* this short scene is one of the film's most memorable moments and that is almost entirely due to this skilled actor's superb employment of second circle of concentration.

Two's company

When there are two principal characters in a film we know that there will be an abundance of wonderful second circle. Edward Albee's brilliantly crafted psychological battle between Richard Burton and Elizabeth Taylor in *Who's Afraid of Virginia Woolf?* demonstrates the devastating power of the second circle. The interplay between 'dentist' Laurence Olivier and Dustin Hoffman in *Marathon Man* will live long in the memory of cinema-goers everywhere with both actors treating us to ample helpings of second circle of concentration. Olivier does this equally brilliantly with Michael Caine in *Sleuth*.

Who's baby?

Fatal Attraction is a marvellous film. There is one scene in particular that sends shivers racing down the spine and it is not the one with the rabbit in the pot! When Glenn Close tells Michael Douglas that she is pregnant and she intends to keep the baby she works the second circle of concentration brilliantly well, giving Douglas so much to work with. She calmly holds his gaze as he races through a series of disturbing emotions – two actors getting the very best out of the circles of concentration.

Having an old friend for dinner

One of the most disturbing deployments of second circle in the cinema came from Anthony Hopkins in *Silence of the Lambs*. It is a classic example of how great writing can build an actor's part by depriving the audience of access to the character for as long as possible. Consequently, when we do meet Hopkins we are not disappointed. The scene begins when Jodie Foster is making her way cell by cell, to confront Hopkins not knowing which cell he is in. At last when we encounter Hopkins standing quite still staring out of his cell, his intense control of second circle of concentration provides one of the most chilling moments in cinema history. None of us will forget the day we met Hannibal Lecter!

Giving the eye

Next time you are told, 'You must have eye contact you know,' remember the second circle of concentration. All of the above are very powerful illustrations of the use of second circle so let's be careful how we use it. We don't want to be engaging people with a Hannibal Lecter style use of focus or connecting with a Lawrence Olivier drill wielding manner either. We need to think about the different ways our eye contact can affect other people and make decisions about the kind of impression we want to have on others. The reason for using our second circle of concentration is generally to connect with people in a positive, friendly, interested and caring way, which in itself carries great power and influence. It's a bit more than just having eye contact. Our eyes are very expressive organs – they say a lot about us and are wonderful instruments for conveying feelings and emotions, wishes and desires, likes and dislikes. They are the window to the soul. So, yes, it is important to have eye contact but let's understand what that can mean. And no wide eyed staring – that's just scary!

Get a grip

Engaging with our audience visually will always be the most memorable form of contact so it is important that we get to grips with all three circles of concentration. With third circle we've acknowledged the bigger picture, and we've seen the power of second circle operating within third. Now we're beginning to piece this focus thing together and pretty soon we will enjoy the benefits of The Clinton Factor.

First circle

How many times has someone said to you, 'I can hear you thinking,' when you have been in a moment of reverie? Plenty no doubt.

The single close up

One of the things we have agreed on at The Speechworks is that it is absolutely fascinating watching someone think. Whether a person is speaking or not, watching them internalize information and process thought is very interesting indeed. This is what the single close up is all about.

The first circle of concentration is the thinking circle. It is the slightly de-focused, introspective circle that acts as a springboard for a new dynamic, a new thought. It is the circle that brings spontaneity to a performance – and let's not forget that all the best told stories are told with spontaneity and enthusiasm.

One to one

Bill Clinton makes great use of first circle, particularly when being interviewed. How many times have we seen politicians answer questions almost before they have finished being asked? You will never see Clinton do this. He will allow an interviewer to finish their question. He will then retreat into his first circle of concentration – sometimes only momentarily – and then give his reply. We believe that he does this if even he does know the answer to the question before the interviewer has finished asking it. The use of first circle in this situation does three things:

1 It pays respect to the person who is asking the question.
2 It acknowledges value in the question being asked.
3 It demonstrates thought and consideration in the response.

Clinton seems to get the measure of first circle absolutely right. Not too little to appear cocksure and not too much to appear self indulgent. We have all witnessed wrong measures of first circle. Too little can actually get to the point where there is none at all and the interviewee gives no value to the question or the person asking it. Too much can give the impression that the interviewee thinks that we are hanging on their every word and are waiting with bated breath for the pearls of wisdom in an over-considered response. First circle must appear genuine.

One for all

We must use first circle of concentration with great care and be most sparing with it. Its use in the interview format is interesting and shows respect. When using first in addressing a larger audience we must choose when to apply it very carefully. We have to bear in mind that in this type of presentation we are supposed to know what we are talking about so overuse of first circle may come across as false and contrived. Careful selection of areas in which to use first circle can be very effective indeed. If we make good decisions in advance about where to use first circle, it will give a freshness and a spontaneity to our performance. The great British comedian Bob Monkhouse, known in the business as The Governor, said that the best spontaneous gags were the well-rehearsed ones. First circle in presentations or speeches works best when it has been pre-selected.

The three Rs: recollection, reflection, reason

There will always be moments in our speeches when we recall, reflect or reason. These moments are great opportunities to employ first circle of concentration. Whether we are remembering, musing or working something out we will invariably be using our first circle of concentration and it's good to let an audience know this – it gives a natural freshness to the delivery.

This is a perfect place to introduce a great example of first circle deployment in a speech. We would like to refer to Colonel Tim Collins again. Recently, an events company invited us to run a series of workshops for a forum of finance directors on board a cruise ship. One of the keynote speakers for the forum was Tim Collins. Tim was speaking about leadership and was making comparisons between leadership in the military and leadership in business. The speech was peppered with anecdotes of incidents of good and bad leadership and its conclusion wrestled with the concern of how many people get the leadership business so badly wrong. This was a great example of a speech using the three Rs. Perfect application of first circle of concentration working in tandem with second and always being in third. This is what can happen when all the components of The Clinton Factor fall into place, the final one being first circle of concentration. We would all like to be able to perform like Tim and Bill and maybe we can if we master the circles of concentration.

Back on screen

Let's stay with first circle and go back to the silver screen. It's important that we can have some good visuals of first circle of concentration to relate to. If we think that second circle of concentration has a powerful effect in film making wait until we see what kind of impact great first circle can have on an audience.

Stolen

Good films like good books and good speeches are all memorable for their beginnings and their ends. One of the finest ends to a movie is in *The Long Good Friday* with Bob Hoskins and Helen Mirren. This is a gangster film set in London in the 1970s with Bob Hoskins playing mobster Harold Shand. Hoskins spends the whole film working out who is trying to kill him and why. In the final scene, when he thinks that things might just be getting back to normal, he is bundled into the back of his own car and kidnapped by the IRA. A young Pierce Brosnan plays his IRA captor and engages Hoskins in a steely second circle from the front seat. The scene is stolen, however, by Hoskins' riveting performance in first circle. In one of the longest single close ups in film history the camera focuses entirely on Hoskins' look of resignation and dread as he is driven to his place of execution and the heart thumping music of Francis Monkman plays us out.

Here's Johnny!

Johnny Depp displays wonderful first circle in the film *Donnie Brasco*. He plays an undercover FBI agent infiltrating the mob in New York. He records all of his conversations with a small tape recorder hidden in his boot. In one scene Depp and his mob colleagues visit a Japanese restaurant where they are asked to remove their shoes. If he does this he knows that his cover will be blown so he invents the story of being raised in an orphanage because his father was killed by the Japanese during the war. In a fit of racism the gang force the manager of the restaurant into the toilet and beat him senseless. It's a very graphic scene that is followed by an extremely still scene where Depp is replaying the tape of the incident in his apartment. The superb choice of single close up reveals a brilliant first circle racked with guilt and fear. This is a marvellous example of how an actor can say nothing but reveal so much.

The last farewell

Lovers of *Inspector Morse* with John Thaw will remember the final episode of the final series which was called 'The Remorseful Day'. In it is a very simple scene where Morse is contemplating his future. A long and slow zoom finds Thaw sitting at home listening to a Schubert string quartet. With the most remarkable and spellbinding use of first circle Thaw lets us into his thoughts about how Morse's career has ended and these are possibly some of the actor's personal thoughts about the end of a long-running series and possibly more coming into play too. A brilliant and powerful piece of acting using first circle. Great stuff!

22

the focus switchers

So we have written, directed and starred in our own movie. We know what this focus business is all about. That maybe so, but perhaps we should remind ourselves by taking a look at a few of the great movies focus switchers. When asked about favourite films a lot of people will list *The Godfather* – some will even say *Godfather 1* and 2. Both great movies with first class scripts and direction, and acted by some of America's best such as Marlon Brando, Robert de Niro, Al Pacino, Diane Keaton, Talia Shire and Robert Duval.

There is a wonderful demonstration of focus switching in The *Godfather 2* when Al Pacino is trying to stop Diane Keaton from leaving him, taking their two daughters with her. Pacino has been hoping that they would have a boy and tells her that she will get over her recent miscarriage and be able to get back to normal and try again. Keaton informs Pacino that she did not have a miscarriage – she had an abortion because she didn't want their son to grow up in his world. The director uses a tight close up on Pacino as he takes in this information. In a matter of a few seconds he switches rapidly back and forth between first and second circle signifying disbelief and confusion before finally exploding with anger. It is one of the most intense and gripping moments in the film and all down to his mastery of the circles of concentration.

There are many great scenes in *Kramer versus Kramer* between Dustin Hoffman and Meryl Streep. One of the best face to face scenes is when Streep returns home to say that their son belongs at home with his father and she is not going to take him with her. Streep moves between first and second circle so skilfully we know exactly what she is feeling – she is sad and frustrated but she is also racked with guilt and shame. We get all of this through her subtle yet superb use of the circles of concentration.

Focus switching can also be used to great comic effect. Hugh Grant has made himself a world expert at this. There is one rather touching scene in *Notting Hill*, however, when Grant uses focus switching to create pathos. Julia Roberts turns up at the book shop to ask Grant for a second chance so they can carry on seeing each other. This is a very static scene where they stand a couple of metres apart and have no physical contact. Grant manages to convey that he has given this some serious thought and has decided it best that they don't see each other any more. His use of first and second circles tells the story in what is one of the film's best scenes. The slightly awkward switching between first and second circle has become one of Grant's trademarks which makes his performances highly watchable. In another marvellous scene from *Notting Hill*, Julia Roberts makes terrific use of second in third when Grant proposes to her at the press conference. Two extremely talented actors getting the very best out of the circles of concentration.

Natural additives

Standing up and speaking in front of people is an unnatural and artificial thing to do and our audiences enjoy the artificiality of the situation. It is our job to bring some normality to the unnatural occasion. We have all heard people say, 'She is such a good speaker – it was as if she was having a normal conversation with us.' If we are to give our audiences the very best we can offer, we need to embrace the first circle of concentration and make it work in all of our addresses. We should not have to search too hard to find places we can use it.

There will, without doubt, be at least one of the three Rs in all of our presentations or speeches. We will always have to recall, reflect or reason with something. In everyday conversations we use first circle naturally. In the artificial situations of our presentations and speeches many of us will not use first circle at all. That is why we must identify areas where we can inject spontaneity – making the artificial natural – the Clinton way.

23

directing the movie

We've done it! We have acquired the three basic shots we need to produce a good movie – the safety shot, the intimate two shot and the single close up – what more do we need? We need to bring them all together in the right measure to grip our audience and steer them through our story. We are a one person production team. We are writer, director, producer and actor. We are ready to make and star in our film – *The Clinton Factor*.

This is where you can score over the actors. You are a one person show. Actors are often at the mercy of bad writing or bad direction, or both. You have more control.

Making your entrance

The script is in its final draft. It has been learned and rehearsed and is ready to shoot. All we need to do now is decide what shots to use and when. Let's assume that we are working a large space with an audience in excess of 50. When we are introduced we need to enter on stage in our third circle of concentration sending out that energy to bring all of our audience into that third circle, never letting them go until we have left the performance space.

We need to take our time. We need to let our audience take us in. We need them to engage with us visually before we begin our opening dialogue. This is the establishing safety shot. Remember Clinton at the O_2 Arena and his performance with his papers and his glasses. A perfectly planned scene to allow the audience to settle and gather their attention.

Perhaps we have chosen a slight moment of first circle before we say our first words, just to bring a degree of spontaneity to our opening remarks, which will draw the audience in and give them confidence in our abilities as a speaker. It will relax them and make them feel at ease with us. They might feel that they are about to witness an off the cuff presentation which always breeds an air of excitement. Once our audience is in this state of calm expectancy, we have them where we want them and we can go to work.

'Action!'

We now deploy our random selection second circle of concentration in a series of intimate two shots always remembering to give an equally spread distribution throughout the space. Every two shot is held for a matter of a few seconds and is then rapidly switched. The rapidity of the distribution should not detract from the even pace of our delivery. It is simply there to share something of ourselves with our audience whilst keeping them in a calm and comfortable state. If we are sufficiently on top of our material we can now begin to analyse the reactions of our audience and make any appropriate adjustments to our delivery. We should now be gaining some confidence in the fact that we have, through second circle, been able to retain a good level of attention from our audience and that they are taking in what we have to say to them.

Second in third is working well and we are really getting into our stride. Time to mix it up a little. Time to use the thinking circle. We are now coming to the first point in our talk when we are ready for our single close up. We will have already identified the pockets in our address where we need to retreat into our first circle of concentration. When we do this there will almost certainly be a natural change of pace. Let's remember that we do not have to think in silence. We can still talk in first circle but the speed of delivery may slow down a little as it does naturally in life. This is what makes things interesting. This is what draws the audience in. We are changing down the gears and our audience are very much in for the ride. As we recall, reflect or reason in first we will be preparing to switch focus to second. This will maintain the freshness of the speech as we engage the audience with a new thought and change our presentation with a different dynamic. As we move back up the gears, perhaps we can fix a point at the back of the space for a moment of pure third! Now we're having fun!

When we are able to harness the circles of concentration and use them with confidence we will have solved the puzzle of The Clinton Factor. This is when what we have to say becomes more interesting. This is when our message becomes memorable. This is when we have a performance!

What the critics say

Did our movie sound a little far fetched? No, certainly not! What we did may not revolutionize movie history but we definitely engaged our audience with our story. Will our movie win any Oscars? Possibly not but it will have entertained and connected in a positive way. Do we care what the critics say? Yes, we do! It's important that our audiences leave to talk about our performance in good terms. The only way we can stand a chance at making a positive impact is to give a powerful performance and that means understanding how to operate our own focus and manage the focus of our audience. It means using the circles. If we do this well we will be talked about with praise. We will rise in the estimation of our peers. We will be used as examples of what is good. What more could we possibly want?

> 'Begin low, speak slow; take fire, rise higher; when most impressed be self-possessed; at the end wax warm, and sit down in a storm.'

Anonymous

On the spot or in the spot?

Practise, practise, practise those circles! The more you apply them the more habitual they will become. This is the best way to boost confidence and lower anxiety. The next time your boss asks you to do his presentation for him the task may not be so daunting. They might not be your words but at least you will have a box of tricks to help you deliver them. When you have mastered the circles of concentration, short notice speaking will not fill you with so much dread – you will be employing The Clinton Factor.

part five summary

In this part you will learn:
- how story combines with status to bring about credibility
- how focus combines with status to bring about presence
- how focus combines with story to create delivery
- how story, status and focus combine to bring about a total performance.

24

grasping the concept

The Clinton Factor is a powerful force yet an easily grasped concept. There aren't many public figures that have the kind of draw that Bill Clinton enjoys and there aren't many figures that one could drape the combined attributes of story, status and focus (SSF) around. A simple choice of example but a most effective one. The wonderful thing about The Clinton Factor is its accessibility – a word we have used a lot in this book. The Clinton Factor is there for everyone to take on board. By accepting that SSF are the main components of great communication we can all change our lives for the better. In our summing up we want to show you how the amalgamation of story, status and focus brings about credibility, presence and delivery – CPD. Here is how it breaks down.

Credibility

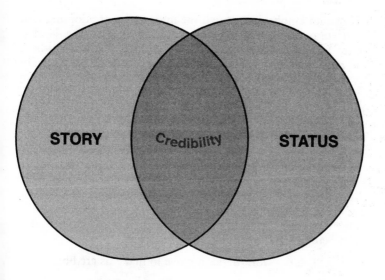

Story and credibility

In any form of communication it is essential that we remain credible at all times. Many of us will have seen speeches and presentations that although slick and polished didn't quite ring true – the bell was cracked. If we don't believe the person speaking is credible, it is not a good speech. Story and status are the key components of credibility. We have said before that if you do not believe in your story then don't tell it – you will be found out. Our material is there to support us and we must believe it to be at least based on fact.

If we believe in what we have to say and the construction of our message complies with everything we have previously said about storytelling, we are a long way to achieving credibility. If we do not believe our story and it is not properly put together, we must go back and start again. The moment we start talking about something we do not entirely believe in, our vocal, physical and emotional status will over-compensate and betray us. When our material is supporting us as it should, we start to feel good about what we are saying which helps with our credibility. Get the story right!

Status and credibility

We cannot emphasize enough the importance of adopting mid-level status for effective communication. The wrong level of status will let us down. If our story is right then we will be in the right frame of mind (mental status) to bring all the good levels of status into play. Our physical status is the first thing our audience will see. An open and neutral physical status will send out the message that we are comfortable and relaxed. It will, in turn, have a reassuring effect on those looking at us. An open and neutral physical status will also have a calming and confidence boosting effect on us. When good physical status is operating then a mid-level vocal status will easily follow – a status that is pitched confidently and strongly without being overpowering. Now our emotional status can truthfully colour our opinion about what we have to say. We will become credible in the eyes of our audience and there will be a greater chance of them being receptive to what we are saying.

Story and status work hand in glove to make us credible.

Presence

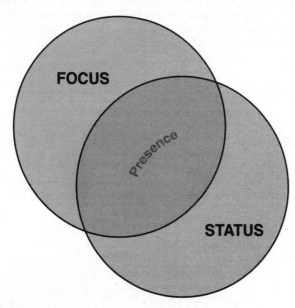

Status and presence

Status and presence are two words that sound well together – indeed some might even confuse one for the other. There can be good and bad presence. Where low or high status is used, there will be bad presence and our audience will switch off. When people say, 'Wow, the speaker had great presence,' it is because mid-level status has been employed. Great presence means our audience has confidence in us as a speaker and that can only be achieved by adopting mid-level status – remember anything else will close us down. Presence is what we need but it must be the right kind of presence and only mid-level status will provide this.

Focus and presence

The right level of status has taken us where we need to be in terms of our presence. Now we can make things more interesting for our audience by applying focus to enhance and maximize the impact of our presence. Back to good old Stan and the circles of concentration.

We used the artist's palette analogy earlier in this book and this is the perfect moment to bring it back. Careful application of focus will bring colour and texture to the presence we have created through adopting the right level of status. The use of the three circles of concentration will bring another dimension to our presence – that's what they are there for. Focus will dictate the varying shades of colour of our presence and complete the picture for our audience – a moving image that we are in complete control of.

Status and focus combine to create the perfect presence.

Delivery

Demosthenes (384–322 BC) was considered by Cicero to be 'the perfect orator' and the three major components of great communication he said were 'delivery, delivery and delivery!'

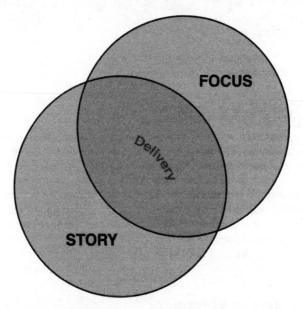

Story and delivery

The story is what we are delivering and it must be in good shape. It is true, of course, that the best delivery in the world will not save bad material and that is why story and delivery have to be the perfect bedfellows. When we construct our story it must always be done with our delivery in mind. This is not a story that we are simply going to read: it has to be performed –

it has to be created with performance in mind. Grammar can go out of the window when we tell our stories. There isn't an audience in the world that will be interested in punctuation when it comes to the telling of a story. Any actor worth their salt will tell you that it doesn't matter how it reads – it is how it plays that is important.

Focus and delivery

What is also important is how the storyteller looks when they are telling the story and how they are working their audience. When we create our stories we should always be mindful of a seemingly random use of focus with which we need to tell those stories. This is why story and focus must work together. Focus and the use of the circles of concentration are the finishing touches to the delivery of any material. Focus will always be the icing on the cake and stories told with a lack of varying focus are incomplete.

Stories are managed with focus.

The three circles of The Clinton Factor: total performance

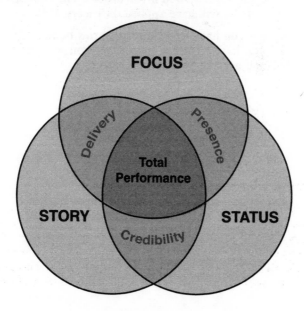

As the guy from the *A Team* used to say, 'I love it when a plan comes together!' Wouldn't it be wonderful to have a total performance? Well, we can – that's what The Clinton Factor is all about. SSF equals a total performance. Yes, easy to put that into a diagram – but it's true. When story, status and focus work together to bring about credibility, presence and delivery, we have a total performance.

There are plenty of people around who will tell you to look smart, stand straight, have eye contact and speak up. Fine, but there's a lot more to it than that. If we concentrate on SSF all of those things will be taken care of plus much, much more. Just look at story, status and focus – that's all we ask. Get the story right, check the level of status, and focus by using the three circles. It couldn't be simpler. SSF may not make you the most powerful person in the world but it will make you a better communicator.

We are living in a world where we are increasingly being asked to stand up and speak. It isn't a prospect that we all relish. It often isn't what we signed up to do and in most cases we would probably rather be anywhere else than in front of an audience. Feelings of anxiety or inadequacy are common and we must confront them. Paying attention to SSF and developing The Clinton Factor will help. SSF is a failsafe foundation to build your public addresses on and if you acquire The Clinton Factor in the process you will have applied the theory well.

We hope that you have enjoyed reading this book and that the next time you have to stand and deliver you will think of us, apply SSF and achieve The Clinton Factor!

appendices

Hillary Rodham Clinton

It would be wrong to write a book about The Clinton Factor without mentioning Hillary. The Clinton Factor – has she got it? Hmmm. If she has it isn't in the genes.

In a recent interview with Eric Schmidt, CEO of Google, he referred to a conversation he had had with Ira Magaziner, Chairman of the Clinton Foundation Policy Board, among other things. Schmidt, who had been working with Bill Clinton on some new software, remarked on how incredibly intelligent the President was. Magaziner replied, 'She's smarter!'

Being smart is good, but having The Clinton Factor would make that smart great. So have any of Bill's enviable qualities rubbed off on Hillary? Well, to be in the running for the most powerful position in the world is no mean feat and Hillary Clinton will have no doubt encountered numerous obstacles throughout her career simply by being female. In education and in the workplace, women of Hillary's age will not have had the easiest of times no matter who they teamed up with. This, we might assume, could lead someone in her place to be over eager to tell her story, to adopt a confrontational level of high status and be rather selfish in her focus. One could possibly understand that kind of single-minded, blinkered determination. One may well forgive a hardnosed cavalier attitude in a woman bent on political success. We might even applaud the achievements of a woman who is going to get there come what may.

Is this what we get from Hillary Rodham Clinton, or is The Clinton Factor in operation? Let's take a look.

Hillary's story

Hillary Clinton's personal story is quite a remarkable one. We did say at the beginning of this book that it is not about politics nor is it a biography. As we are covering the subjects of SSF, however, we do need to relate those areas to the performance of Hillary Clinton and her telling of her own story does the right things as far as we are concerned regarding storytelling. In fact the majority of her messages appear to be well constructed, concisely edited and told with passion and conviction.

Her speeches seem to be strong and heartfelt. They are punchy and get to the point. There is a refreshing directness in her public addresses which is possibly because of having to compete in what has been very much a male-dominated arena for many years. When it comes to getting attention with a well-edited and well-told story, Hilary is no slouch. The world of politics is fuelled by narrative and Hillary Clinton has recognized the importance of getting it right. There is obviously a very bright and quick mind operating and this is quite apparent when we see her in the interview situation. To do what is necessary to engage all of the mechanics needed to create and tell a good story when improvizing is not easy, but Hillary seems to have a very good handle on these situations, which is down to her honed ability to construct, edit and deliver on the hoof. So, with regard to the first element of SSF – story – she is doing well.

Status and Hillary

As you now know, status and adopting the right level of status is at the very heart of every piece of successful communication. If Hillary does not shape up in this department there is simply no going forward for her. Great leaders need to be in touch with those they represent. Great leaders need to be attuned to the needs and desires of the electorate. Great leaders need to be able to open their arms and let us in!

So does she get it right? Let's break it down.

Physical Hillary

Hillary is actually very good physically and she seems to grow in physical confidence. Nobody could ever accuse her of being of low physical status – and she stays away from the other extreme very well. After watching hours of Hillary on video we can quite confidently say that she is definitely in the 5 to 7 channel – the Clinton channel. Small in stature (unlike Bill) – big in presence (like Bill). There appears to be a very relaxed physicality with Hillary, which, of course, makes an audience feel comfortable. When we see Hillary on her feet, there is no doubt that we are watching a performer, which is what every audience wants. There is, however, a gesture problem.

What do I do with my hands?

As little as possible! Sit on 'em! Put 'em in your pockets! Chop 'em off – damn it! Seriously, though, Hillary does have a gesture problem and, let's face it, don't most of us? Over-gesticulation can detract from what could otherwise be a great physical performance. Although her gestures are appropriate to her words they are excessive. She is at home and at her best with gestures when they are open and expansive – but she lets herself down with over-use of the chopping motion which can very easily take us into high physical status territory. The good thing about Hillary's gesticulation problem is that the gestures appear to be generated by genuine belief. Nevertheless, it is definitely something to be aware of and she should address the issue of speaking too much with her hands.

Generally speaking, Hillary's physical status sends out a positive signal that this is someone who is relaxed and in charge. Our physical status is almost always the first thing we are judged upon – she is definitely on the right track.

Vocal Hillary

At breakfast, in response to the Bishop's suggestion that the curate had a bad egg the latter replied – 'Parts of it are excellent!' (from a *Punch* cartoon by Geroge Du Maurier called 'True Humility'). Hillary's vocal image is a little bit like the curate's egg.

The home of the brave and the land of the free

We could not have a section in this book titled 'Vocal Hillary' without addressing her destruction of the National Anthem. After watching many hours of Hillary on tape came the climax of our Hillary research – her recent rendition of the Anthem. We watched open mouthed only to conclude that if she hit one correct note it was probably a fluke! Which is, no doubt, why she chose a career in politics rather than light opera.

The Clinton cackle

Apparently coined by friends of Clinton, 'The Clinton cackle' has been much reported by those in opposition as signs of defensiveness and being forced. Even former Bill Clinton adviser Dick Morris described Hillary's laugh as 'loud, inappropriate, and mirthless... A scary sound that was somewhere between a cackle and a screech.'

The Clintons do enjoy a laugh. That was no more apparent than when Bill had his almost uncontrollable burst of merriment at Boris Yeltsin's put down of a US journalist at a joint press conference. You can view this for yourself on YouTube by typing 'Clinton and Yeltsin' into the search field. It is well worth taking a look at this clip of genuine uncontrollable corpsing. It was spontaneous and very funny – people in the public eye do, however, need to monitor their mirth. Whilst laughter can be a good part of a vocal image, it can also have an adverse effect if it is too loud, too harsh or simply comes out at the wrong time.

Hillary has quite a variety of laughs in her repertoire including the rather endearing Clinton chortle but the Clinton cackle needs to be kept in check. A loud and raucous laugh in a social situation can be quite amusing, even contagious, but in the cut and thrust of serious politics it probably will not have the same appeal. Hillary needs to have better management of the Clinton cackle and save it for more private moments lest it come across as contrived, calculated or, as Patrick Healy of the *New York Times* put it, 'a reaction to pressure'.

Hillary's PTSV

Sometimes Hillary takes a while to settle down vocally, particularly in the interview situation. She often starts at a generally high level of vocal status before finding her way into the more acceptable mid-level. This is probably due to the first minute or two of nerves that most of us feel when we are on show. The not so mellow tone, the higher pitch and the full volume often betray our anxiety in these opening moments. When Hillary gets into her comfort zone she uses her voice very well.

Pitch

There are two very distinct areas of difference when it comes to Hillary's pitch. In the uninterrupted centre stage address her pitch is raised to the higher end of mid-level status, which gives off excitement and anticipation without pushing an audience away. In interview her pitch has a little more variety as one might expect in a less heightened more conversational situation. If some of her interview pitch variety could cross over into her on stage delivery her overall vocal image would be enhanced.

Tone

Rather like her messages, Hillary's tone could be described as strong and direct. Unlike Bill's somewhat mellifluous tones, she has more of an edge which can have a positive effect in certain circumstances. This edge can, however, act as a barrier and keep an audience at a distance. Perhaps Hillary should take a closer look at Bill's tonality – this would, no doubt, increase her accessibility to those she wishes to reach.

Speed

The speed of Hillary's delivery is fine – a little quicker than Bill's but he does have a rather enviable relaxed and laid back delivery in all of his communication. Hillary has more variety in the pace of her delivery than Bill which is in keeping with her character. It is important that the pace of our delivery is indicative of our personalities without letting it veer towards the extremes.

Volume

As we said earlier, Hillary's volume generally (Clinton cackle aside) can be a little on the high side of mid-level vocal status. This is fine when on stage in front of a large audience but somewhat overwhelming in a studio situation. When she settles into the surroundings and their atmosphere she is able to adjust her volume and, indeed, vary it for emphasis. Bill, on the other hand, finds a comfortable level of volume very quickly in virtually any situation.

Emotional Hillary

We have said earlier that emotional status is probably the most important component of The Clinton Factor. It is, therefore, crucial that Hillary is in command of her emotional status to be able to communicate effectively. The talent of being able to listen to, attune to and respond to the needs and desires of others is absolutely vital to people aspiring to be great leaders.

Hillary at the podium

The stand-alone delivery situation is probably the easiest environment in which to manage our emotional status. It is a platform for us to display how we feel, how we understand and how we intend to make a difference. It is an opportunity for us to play on the emotions of our audience and sway the mob. This is where great leaders throughout history are remembered – when they can get up for as long as they want and say what they want without major fear of interruption. How does Hillary fare here? Well, pretty good actually. Hillary can work a crowd with the best of them. She is able to harness the right levels of status in other areas to assist her delivery. She does this with confidence and purpose, and with great effect. So what about a tougher challenge?

Hillary in the chair

The interview situation. This is where things can get a little tricky especially if the interviewee is not thoroughly prepared. We've all seen those horrible edgy moments where interviewees fumble, stumble and flounder. From the footage we have seen of Hillary in the chair, she has, on the whole, fared pretty well and managed to use the appropriate degrees of emotion most of the time. She appears to have made some good choices of where to show passion and be empathic. There is, however, one particular reaction that lets Hillary down. We return to the Clinton cackle. A loud burst of raucous laughter can so easily send out the wrong signal and can be quickly interpreted as not taking the subject seriously or even mocking the person asking the question. Best not use it at all Hillary!

Crying Clinton

We couldn't possibly talk about Hillary and emotional status without mentioning the 'crying' incident just prior to the New Hampshire primary in January 2008. Much was made of her teary performance and some were sceptical of how genuine it was. We played this bit of footage time and time again and came up with the following thoughts:

- What a great piece of timing – just after a pretty clear-cut defeat by Obama in Iowa.
- What a great choice of words to force through the tears and qualify the sincerity of the emotion.
- What a great idea to let the American people know that you are only human and are emotionally in tune with the important things in life.

The above comments may appear somewhat cynical. Showing emotion in this way clearly did Hillary a great favour and her fortunes in the New Hampshire primary were reversed. After very close examination it appeared to us that her tug on the emotional heartstrings was genuine and spontaneous – two major qualities of The Clinton Factor. If it was not we were witnessing a master class in acting emotion. If that was the case and Hillary was not successful in furthering her political career in Washington, she could certainly move to Hollywood and take up a career in the movies.

Overall opinion on Hillary and emotional status? Yes, she's getting it right and is moving up to join Bill.

Hillary and focus

We think it is fair to say that Hillary Clinton has been very focused on her career and work in every area but does she employ the three circles of concentration in her public addresses?

Hillary in third

The third circle of concentration is where Hillary Clinton is most at home. She seems to revel in the big address. The bigger the audience the better. She appears to be completely comfortable speaking to large numbers of people and she has no problem sending out that energy of third circle and occupying the performance space with her presence. Hilary Clinton is always in her third circle of concentration, which is, of course, absolutely where she should be when in the public arena. A lot of people don't get anywhere near that. This is a huge plus for her. As we said before – when speaking to large numbers of people, you can almost get by in third alone.

Even when in the more intimate interview situation, Hillary appears to be aware of the importance of third circle of concentration. She understands that although she is talking to one person she is actually addressing millions.

Hillary in second

Yes, she is definitely functioning well in second circle too. She gives an even distribution of her second circle, as far as it is possible, to large audiences. She also engages well in second in smaller gatherings or in the interview environment. Hillary is certainly not afraid of eye contact and there is no manipulative mid-level status that can creep into second circle either. Hillary and second circle are working well together.

Hillary in first

Ah, now here's the rub. Is Hillary using her first circle of concentration as well as she could? Maybe not. She is definitely using first circle but we are talking about The Clinton Factor here so we have to ask the question of whether or not it is up to Bill's high standard and Bill is one of the world's grand masters of first circle of concentration. Hillary is clearly adept at the use of first circle but there is room for her to take the technique further. She knows when to employ first and is skilled in its execution but doesn't appear yet to have had the courage to take it to its limit. Bill knows the limit of first circle and is abundantly talented in taking it to the wire every time. It is a fine art timing a line in first circle or departing from it. We don't think that Hillary has yet mastered her husband's majestic use of first circle.

Conclusion – has she got it or not?

We approached the issue of Hillary and The Clinton Factor with some concern. If she hasn't got it – well, we just have to say that. If she has got it, does that take the spotlight that we are shining on Bill away from him? In order to establish whether or not Hillary has The Clinton Factor and is using SSF to great effect, we watched hours of Hillary on camera. We agreed that she definitely does have The Clinton Factor – but to what degree? TCF cannot be genetic as far as Hillary is concerned but the principles of SSF can be acquired by anybody. Hillary Clinton, consciously or not, applies SSF to her communications exceptionally well. There is also a great degree of The Clinton Factor at play too. (It is, of course, very possible that Hillary has absorbed some of it by proximity.) One has to wonder how that might grow as her public life develops.

Story, status, focus – and PowerPoint®

Bill Clinton has probably never had to make a presentation using PowerPoint® but if he did he would certainly apply SSF. The advent of PowerPoint® changed the world of business presentations. There are some that are able to embrace that technology and make it work for them; there are others that have used it as a screen to hide behind; and there are yet others who expect nothing less from a presentation than a barrage of overheads packed with text and handouts offering the same.

PowerPoint® presentation or presenting with PowerPoint®?

There is a big difference. A common mistake when using PowerPoint® is to assume that it is going to do all the work for us. Wrong! PowerPoint® will not give the presentation for us. We are still the presenter and PowerPoint® is merely there to assist us with our presentation and that means that we have to engage with our audience and manage their focus in the time honoured human way. Presentations are a personal thing that people engage in. Presentations are communicating with speech. Making a presentation involves personally connecting with our audience. Technology is a wonderful thing and it helps us in many ways but there will never be a substitute for the human element in a presentation – PowerPoint® is our glamorous assistant.

Send me your presentation

Heard this one before? Of course you have and hopefully you will have said, 'No! Come and see it!' As soon as you send your presentation to someone else it ceases to be a presentation and becomes an email. An email that will probably go unread if indeed it is downloaded in the first place.

'If I send you my presentation can you do it for me Wednesday morning?' Get out of here! You might as well show someone else's holiday snaps! It's personal! It's our own creation – and if it's not, it jolly well should be. This is where presenting with PowerPoint® can fall down. PowerPoint® is there to support our story. Yes, that's *our* story not someone else's story.

Put it all on the screen

'That's the great thing about PowerPoint® – you don't have to remember it – just put it up there and read it!' Well if that's how it works we might as well email it – at least people will able to read it at their leisure and at their own speed.

'Will there be handouts?' is often asked. 'Yes, everyone will get a printed copy of my slides.' Let's deliver the presentation three times just in case our audience don't get it the first or second time. What madness! Guess what? It gets even crazier! Let's give the audience the handouts as they come into the room, then they can hear it, see it and read it all at the same time! There is a school of thought that says let's tell the audience three times so the message hits home – 'tell 'em what you're going to tell 'em, then tell 'em, then tell 'em what you've told 'em.' We don't disagree with this but putting text on screen, reading the text off the screen and handing out paper copies of the same is taking that adage too literally and will have the opposite result to the one desired. The mind is simply not capable of taking in the same information in different formats at the same time.

Cinema or theatre?

On one of our training days we decided to attack the subject of PowerPoint® by creating our own presentation to see how our coaches reacted to it. All of our crew were familiar with the mode of presentation except for one who sat with a puzzled expression. She eventually asked us to stop and said, 'Sorry –

but am I in the cinema or the theatre? Where am I supposed to be looking?' We were clearly not managing her focus well at all. PowerPoint® is one of the trickiest methods of presentation when it comes to managing the focus of an audience.

Stand up and be counted

This business of assuming that PowerPoint® is going to do the work for us has gone far too far. There appears to be a dangerous belief that we don't even have to stand up if we are presenting with PowerPoint®. One of our clients was about to give a crucial presentation to his board of directors and wanted us to take a look at what he was doing. We asked one of our coaches to go through the presentation with him. Our client sat next to our coach, opened his laptop and started the presentation. The dialogue that followed went something like this:

Coach: Aren't you going to stand up?

Client: No. I thought this would make it kind of relaxed and informal.

Coach: Okay, if we're going to be relaxed and informal, why don't we go round to Starbucks and do it in there – at least the coffee will be better!

Wait, it gets worse! We were asked by a leading marketing company to give a talk at a briefing day for a major new campaign they were undertaking. We arrived on time to do our bit but the day was running a little late so we were invited to sit in on the presentation that was happening. Something was odd. We could hear a voice but could not see who was speaking. It turned out that the presenter was sitting directly in front of us with a microphone looking at the screen and to make matters even worse what she was saying would often not correspond to what we were looking at because she wasn't even pressing the buttons – someone else was doing that! If a leading marketing company can get things so badly wrong what hope is there? Plenty, if you use SSF and The Clinton Factor.

Don't turn your back on me!

Bad use of PowerPoint® has given birth to a whole generation of people who present with their backs. Most of the time this is because they simply haven't bothered to learn their presentation and are reading it from the screen. Sometimes it is because they have allowed themselves to be as distracted by what is on the screen as their audience has. Either way it is a gross mismanagement of focus.

One of our clients had a strange tendency to indicate things on the screen by reaching across himself no matter which side of the screen he stood. This caused him to turn his back on us. The only way we were able to stop this was by getting him to put his outside hand in his pocket. You will, no doubt, have been told never to put your hands in your pockets. Well, if you have this problem – break the rule! It will take care of bad focus straight away and you can always wean yourself off it in time.

Get the picture?

There seems to be a weird theory that the more slides we show the better the presentation. Nothing could be further from the truth. If someone in your organization tells you that they've got a great idea and a 150 slide presentation to prove it – run a mile! Just like the well-edited story, less is more. The more you show the less people will take in.

The triangular relationship

Audience, presenter, screen. It's a three-way thing. The important thing with PowerPoint® is to be mindful of where the audience focus needs to be at any one time. It is entirely up to you. You are in control. You are at the pivotal corner of this strange triangular relationship.

It may seem that we have a huge downer on PowerPoint® – this is not true. We believe that PowerPoint® is a tremendously effective piece of kit when used well. Below are a few tips to presenting with PowerPoint®.

We said earlier that if Clinton presented with PowerPoint® he would certainly employ SSF – we should do the same.

Story and PowerPoint®

We will always be telling a story. Even with analytical information on screen we are telling a story. The overheads are merely there to assist the telling of that story.

Our story needs to be well structured – we need to find our end – we need to know what our objective is before we can work backwards to create the right framework. What is our final slide?

Less is more. If we want our message to be memorable we must limit the information to the essential. Do the five-minute test. If I had to tell this story in five minutes what would I chop out?

Is the story fluid? Is my choice of slides flowing seamlessly from one to the other, and telling my story?

Status and PowerPoint®

Don't close down. Just because there is information on a screen you can still be seen. Use that open and accessible neutral physical status.

Make yourself heard. We may be looking at a screen but what you have to say is still the most important part of your presentation. Select the right level of vocal status for the job to bring light and shade to your presentation.

Empathise. Stay attuned. Let your audience know how you feel about the information you are giving them. Think about your emotional status. Don't just read it!

Focus and PowerPoint®

Stay in control. If you want the audience's focus on screen then direct it there whilst remaining physically open and accessible.

If you want your audience's focus to be on you steer them your way by turning your back on the screen. Don't just look at them – face them!

If you don't want your audience to look at the screen put up a holding slide or a blank slide.

Use the circles. Because you have a screen behind you there will be a danger that you may neglect your third circle of concentration. Be careful – we must never leave our third circle.

There are many areas of business that PowerPoint® lends itself to brilliantly well: analytical businesses that have to identify the ebb and flow of trends in the marketplace; the world of finance where it is necessary to demonstrate figures through charts and graphs; the medical world where diagrams are essential.

By all means use PowerPoint® whatever your business, but use it well – use it with SSF.

Memorable speeches

'I Believe in a Place Called Hope'

This is Bill Clinton's famous speech accepting the Presidential Nomination at the Democratic National Convention in New York 1992

It is passionate speech about hope for the future in which we see a consummate performer still honing his speaking talents. Full of spontaneity and life, using emotional status to enormous effect yet still remaining in the 5–7 Clinton channel. Bright and energetic with a great distribution of personal focus. It is one of Clinton's finest speeches.

Governor Richards, Chairman Brown, Mayor Dinkins, our great host, and my fellow Americans.

I am so proud of Al Gore. He said he came here tonight because he always wanted to do the warmup for Elvis. Well, I ran for President this year for one reason and one reason only: I wanted to come back to this convention center and finish that speech I started four years ago.

Well, last night Mario Cuomo taught us how a real nominating speech should be given. He also made it clear why we have to steer our ship of state on a new course.

Tonight I want to talk with you about my hope for the future, my faith in the American people, and my vision of the kind of country we can build, together.

I salute the good men who were my companions on the campaign trail: Tom Harkin, Bob Kerrey, Doug Wilder, Jerry Brown and Paul Tsongas. One sentence in the platform we built says it all: 'The most important family policy, urban policy, labor policy, minority policy and foreign policy America can have is an expanding, entrepreneurial economy of high-wage, high-skill jobs.'

And so, in the name of all the people who do the work, pay the taxes, raise the kids and play by the rules, in the name of the hard-working Americans who make up our forgotten middle class, I accept your nomination for President of the United States.

I am a product of that middle class. And when I am President you will be forgotten no more.

We meet at a special moment in history, you and I. The Cold War is over; Soviet Communism has collapsed; and our values – freedom, democracy, individual rights and free enterprise – they have triumphed all around the world. And yet just as we have won the Cold War abroad, we are losing the battles for economic opportunity and social justice here at home. Now that we have changed the world, it's time to change America.

I have news for the forces of greed and the defenders of the status quo: your time has come – and gone. It's time for a change in America.

Tonight ten million of our fellow Americans are out of work. Tens of millions more work harder for lower pay. The incumbent President says unemployment always goes up a little before a recovery begins. But unemployment only has to go up by one more person before a real recovery can begin. And, Mr. President, you are that man.

This election is about putting power back in your hands and putting government back on your side. It's about putting people first.

You know, I've said that all across the country, and someone always comes back at me, as a young man did just this week at the Henry Street Settlement on the Lower East Side of Manhattan. He said, 'That sounds good, Bill. But you're a politician. Why should I trust you?'

Tonight, as plainly as I can, I want to tell you who I am, what I believe, and where I want to lead America.

I never met my father. He was killed in a car wreck on a rainy road three months before I was born, driving home from Chicago to Arkansas to see my mother. After that, my mother had to support us. So we lived with my grandparents while she went back to Louisiana to study nursing.

I can still see her clearly tonight through the eyes of a three-year-old: kneeling at the railroad station and weeping as she put me back on the train to Arkansas with my grandmother. She endured her pain because she knew her sacrifice was the only way she could support me and give me a better life.

My mother taught me. She taught me about family and hard work and sacrifice. She held steady through tragedy after tragedy. And she held our family, my brother and I, together through tough times. As a child, I watched her go off to work each day at a time when it wasn't always easy to be a working mother.

As an adult, I've watched her fight off breast cancer. And again she has taught me a lesson in courage. And always, always she taught me to fight.

That's why I'll fight to create high-paying jobs so that parents can afford to raise their children today. That's why I'm so committed to making sure every American gets the health care that saved my mother's life, and that women's health care gets the same attention as men's. That's why I'll fight to make sure women in this country receive respect and dignity – whether they work in the home, out of the home, or both. You want to know where I get my fighting spirit? It all started with my mother.

Thank you, Mother. I love you.

When I think about opportunity for all Americans, I think about my grandfather.

He ran a country store in our little town of Hope. There were no food stamps back then, so when his customer – whether they were white or black, who worked hard and did the best they could, came in with no money – well, he gave them food anyway – just made a note of it. So did I. Before I was big enough to see over the counter, I learned from him to look up to people other folks looked down on.

My grandfather just had a grade-school education. But in that country store he taught me more about equality in the eyes of the Lord than all my professors at Georgetown; more about the intrinsic worth of every individual than all the philosophers at Oxford; and he taught me more about the need for equal justice than all the jurists at Yale Law School.

If you want to know where I come by the passionate commitment I have to bringing people together without regard to race, it all started with my grandfather.

I learned a lot from another person, too. A person who for more than 20 years has worked hard to help our children – paying the price of time to make sure our schools don't fail them. Someone who traveled our state for a year, studying, learning, listening, going to PTA meetings, school board meetings, town hall meetings, putting together a package of school reforms recognized around the nation, and doing it all while building a distinguished legal career and being a wonderful loving mother.

That person is my wife.

Hillary taught me. She taught me that all children can learn, and that each of us has a duty to help them do it. So if you want to know why I care so much about our children and our future; it all started with Hillary. I love you.

Frankly, I'm fed up with politicians in Washington lecturing the rest of us about 'family values.' Our families have values. But our government doesn't.

I want an America where 'family values' live in our actions, not just in our speeches – an America that includes every family, every traditional family and every extended family, every two-parent family, every single-parent family, and every foster family – every family.

I do want to say something to the fathers in this country who have chosen to abandon their children by neglecting to pay their child support: take responsibility for your children or we will force you to do so. Because governments don't raise children; parents do. And you should.

And I want to say something to every child in America tonight who is out there trying to grow up without a father or a mother: I know how you feel. You're special, too. You matter to America. And don't ever let anybody tell you you can't become whatever you want to be. And if other politicians make you feel like you're not a part of their family, come on and be part of ours.

The thing that makes me angriest about what's gone wrong in the last 12 years is that our government has lost touch with our values, while our politicians continue to shout about them. I'm tired of it.

I was raised to believe its that the American Dream was built on rewarding hard work. But we have seen the folks in Washington turn the American ethic on its head. For too long, those who play by the rules and keep the faith have gotten the shaft, and those who cut corners and cut deals have been rewarded. People are working harder than ever, spending less time with their children, working nights and weekends at their jobs instead of gong to PTA and Little League or Scouts, and their incomes are still going down. Their taxes are going up, and the costs of health care, housing and education are going through the roof. Meanwhile, more and more of our best people are falling into poverty – even when they work forty hours a week.

Our people are pleading for change, but government is in the way. It has been hijacked by privileged, private interests. It has forgotten who really pays the bills around here – it's taking more of your money and giving you less in return.

We have got to go beyond the brain-dead politics in Washington, and give our people the kind of government they deserve: a government that works for them.

A President – a President ought to be a powerful force for progress. But right now I know how President Lincoln felt when General McClellan wouldn't attack in the Civil War. He asked him, 'If you're not going to use your army, may I borrow it?' And so I say, George Bush, if you won't use your power to help America, step aside. I will.

Our country is falling behind. The President is caught in the grip of a failed economic theory. We have gone from first to thirteenth in the world in wages since Reagan and Bush have been in office. Four years ago, candidate Bush said America is a special place, not just 'another pleasant country on the UN roll call, between Albania and Zimbabwe.' Now, under President Bush, America has an unpleasant economy stuck somewhere between Germany and Sri Lanka. And for most Americans, Mr. President, life's a lot less kind and a lot less gentle than it was before your Administration took office.

Our country has fallen so far, so fast that just a few months ago the Japanese Prime Minister actually said he felt 'sympathy' for the United States. Sympathy. When I am your President, the rest of the world will not look down on us with pity, but up to us with respect again.

What is George Bush doing about our economic problems? Now, four years ago he promised us fifteen million new jobs by this time. And he's over fourteen million short. Al Gore and I can do better.

He has raised taxes on the people driving pick-up trucks, and lowered taxes on people riding in limousines. We can do better.

He promised to balance the budget, but he hasn't even tried. In fact, the budgets he has submitted have nearly doubled the debt. Even worse, he wasted billions and reduced our investment in education and jobs. We can do better.

So if you are sick and tired of a government that doesn't work to create jobs; if you're sick and tired of a tax system that's stacked against you; if you're sick and tired of exploding debt and reduced investments in our future – or if, like the great civil rights pioneer Fannie Lou Hamer, you're just plain old sick and tired of being sick and tired – then join us, work with us, win with us. And we can make our country the country it was meant to be.

Now, George Bush talks a good game. But he has no game plan to rebuild America from the cities to the suburbs to the countryside so that we can compete and win again in the global economy. I do.

He won't take on the big insurance companies and the bureaucracies to control health costs and give us affordable health care for all Americans. But I will.

He won't even implement the recommendations of his own Commission on AIDS. But I will.

He won't streamline the federal government, and change the way it works; cut a hundred thousand bureaucrats, and put a hundred thousand new police officers on the streets of American cities. But I will.

He has never balanced a government budget. But I have, eleven times.

He won't break the stranglehold the special interests have on our elections and the lobbyists have on our government. But I will.

He won't give mothers and fathers the simple chance to take some time off from work when a baby is born or a parent is sick. But I will.

We're losing our family farms at a rapid rate, and he has no commitment to keep family farms in the family. But I do.

He's talked a lot about drugs, but he hasn't helped people on the front line to wage that war on drugs and crime. But I will.

He won't take the lead in protecting the environment and creating new jobs in environmental technology. But I will.

You know what else? He doesn't have Al Gore and I do.

Just in case – just in case you didn't notice, that's Gore with an E on the end.

And George Bush – George Bush won't guarantee a woman's right to choose. I will. Listen, hear me now: I am not pro-abortion. I am pro-choice strongly. I believe this difficult and painful decision should be left to the women of America. I hope the right to privacy can be protected, and we will never again have to discuss this issue on political platforms. But I am old enough to remember what it was like before *Roe v. Wade*. And I do not want to return to the time when we made criminals of women and their doctors.

Jobs. Education. Health care. These are not just commitments from my lips. They are the work of my life.

Our priorities must be clear: we will put our people first again. But priorities without a clear plan of action are just empty words. To turn our rhetoric into reality we've got to change the way government does business – fundamentally. Until we do, we'll continue to pour billions of dollars down the drain.

The Republicans have campaigned against big government for a generation. But have you noticed? They've run this big government for a generation. And they haven't changed a thing. They don't want to fix government. They still want to campaign against it, and that's all.

But, my fellow Democrats, it's time for us to realize that we've got some changing to do too. There is not a program in government for every problem. And if we want to use government to help people, we've got to make it work again.

Because we are committed in this convention and in this platform to making these changes, we are, as Democrats, in the words that Ross Perot himself spoke today, a revitalized Democratic party. I am well aware that all those millions of people who rallied to Ross Perot's cause wanted to be in an army of patriots for change. Tonight I say to them: join us and together we will revitalize America.

Now, I don't have all the answers. But I do know the old ways don't work. Trickle down economics has sure failed. And big bureaucracies, both private and public, they've failed, too.

That's why we need a new approach to government – a government that offers more empowerment and less entitlement, more choices for young people in the schools they attend, in the public schools they attend, and more choices for the elderly and for people with disabilities and the long-term care they receive – a government that is leaner, not meaner. A government that expands opportunity, not bureaucracy – a government that understands that jobs must come from growth in a vibrant and vital system of free enterprise. I call this approach a New Covenant – a solemn agreement between the people and their government – based not simply on what each of us can take but on what all of us must give to our nation.

We offer our people a new choice based on old values. We offer opportunity. We demand responsibility. We will build an American community again. The choice we offer is not conservative or liberal. In many ways it's not even Republican or Democratic, It's different. It's new. And it will work.

It will work because it is rooted in the vision and the values of the American people. Of all the things George Bush has ever said that I disagree with, perhaps the thing that bothers me most is how he derides and degrades the American tradition of seeing – and seeking – a better future. He mocks it as 'the vision thing.' But remember just what the Scripture says: 'Where there is no vision the people perish.'

I hope – I hope nobody in this great hall tonight or in our beloved country has to go through tomorrow without a vision. I hope no one ever tries to raise a child without a vision. I hope nobody ever starts a business or plants a crop in the ground without a vision – for where there is no vision the people perish.

One of the reasons we have so many children in so much trouble in so many places in this nation is because they have seen so little opportunity, so little responsibility, and so little loving, caring community that they literally cannot imagine the life we are calling them to lead. And so I say again, where there is no vision America will perish.

What is the vision of our New Covenant?

An America with millions of new jobs in dozens of new industries moving confidently toward the 21st Century. An

America that says to entrepreneurs and business people: We will give you more incentives and more opportunity than ever before to develop the skills of your workers and create American jobs and American wealth in the new global economy. But you must do your part; you must be responsible. American companies must act like American companies again – exporting products, not jobs. That's what this New Covenant is all about.

An America in which the doors of college are thrown open once again to the sons and daughters of stenographers and steelworkers. We'll say: Everybody can borrow the money to go to college. But you must do your part. You must pay it back – from your paychecks, or better yet, by going back home and serving your communities. Just think of it. Think of it; millions of energetic young men and women, serving their country by policing the streets, or teaching the children or caring for the sick, or working with the elderly or people with disabilities, or helping young people to stay off drugs and out of gangs, giving us all a sense of new hope and limitless possibilities. That's what this New Covenant is all about.

An America in which health care is a right, not a privilege. In which we say to all of our people: Your government has the courage – finally – to take on the health care profiteers and make health care affordable for every family. But you must do your part: preventive care, prenatal care, childhood immunization; saving lives, saving money, saving families from heartbreak. That's what the New Covenant is all about.

An America in which middle class incomes – not middle class taxes – are going up. An America, yes, in which the wealthiest few – those making over $200,000 a year – are asked to pay their fair share. An America in which the rich are not soaked – but the middle class is not drowned either. Responsibility starts at the top; that's what the New Covenant is all about.

An America where we end welfare as we know it. We will say to those on welfare: you will have and you deserve the opportunity through training and education, through child care and medical coverage, to liberate yourself. But then, when you can, you must work, because welfare should be a second chance, not a way of life. That's what the New Covenant is all about.

An America with the world's strongest defense; ready and willing to use force, when necessary. An America at the forefront of the global effort to preserve and protect our common environment – and promoting global growth.

An America that will not coddle tyrants, from Baghdad to Beijing. An America that champions the cause of freedom and democracy, from Eastern Europe to Southern Africa, and in our own hemisphere in Haiti and Cuba.

The end of the Cold War permits us to reduce defense spending while still maintaining the strongest defense in the world. But we must plow back every dollar of defense cuts into building American jobs right here at home. I know well that the world needs a strong America, but we have learned that strength begins at home.

But the New Covenant is about more than opportunities and responsibilities for you and your families. It's also about our common community. Tonight every one of you knows deep in your heart that we are too divided.

It is time to heal America. And so we must say to every American: look beyond the stereotypes that blind us. We need each other. All of us, we need each other. We don't have a person to waste. And yet, for too long, politicians have told the most of us that are doing all right that what's really wrong with America is the rest of us. Them. Them the minorities. Them the liberals. Them the poor. Them the homeless. Them the people with disabilities. Them the gays. We've gotten to where we've nearly them'd ourselves to death. Them, and them, and them. But this is America. There is no them; there is only us. One nation, under God, indivisible, with liberty, and justice, for all.

That is our Pledge of Allegiance, and that's what the New Covenant is all about.

How do I know we can come together to make change happen? Because I have see it in my own state. In Arkansas we're working together and we're making progress. No, there is no Arkansas miracle. But there are a lot of miraculous people. And because of them, our schools are better, our wages are higher, our factories are busier, our water is cleaner, and our budget is balanced. We're moving ahead.

I wish – I wish I could say the same thing about America under the incumbent President. He took the richest country in the world and brought it down. We took one of the poorest states in America and lifted it up.

And so I say to those who would criticize Arkansas: come on

down. Especially if you're from Washington – come to Arkansas. You'll see us struggling against some problems we haven't solved yet. But you'll also see a lot of great people doing amazing things. And you might even learn a thing or two.

In the end, the New Covenant simply asks us all to be Americans again – old-fashioned Americans for a new time. Opportunity. Responsibility. Community. When we pull together, America will pull ahead. Throughout the whole history of this country, we have seen time and again that when we are united, we are unstoppable. We can seize this moment, we can make it exciting and energizing and heroic to be an American again. We can renew our faith in ourselves and each other, and restore our sense of unity and community. Scripture says, our eyes have not yet seen, nor our ears heard, nor our minds imagined what we can build.

But I cannot do it alone. No President can. We must do it together. It won't be easy and it won't be quick. We didn't get into this mess overnight, and we won't get out of it overnight. But we can do it – with our commitment and our creativity and our diversity and our strength. I want every person in this hall and every citizen in this land to reach out and join us in a great new adventure to chart a bold new future.

As a teenager I heard John Kennedy's summons to citizenship. And then, as a student at Georgetown, I heard that call clarified by a professor I had, named Carroll Quigley, who said America was the greatest country in the history of the world because our people have always believed in two great ideas: first, that tomorrow can be better than today, and second, that each of us has a personal, moral responsibility to make it so.

That future entered my life the night our daughter Chelsea was born. As I stood in that delivery room, I was overcome with the thought that God had given me a blessing my own father never knew: the chance to hold my child in my arms.

Somewhere at this very moment, another child is born in America. Let it be our cause to give that child a happy home, a healthy family, a hopeful future. Let it be our cause to see that child reach the fullest of her God-given abilities. Let it be our cause that she grow up strong and secure, braced by her challenges, but never, never struggling alone; with family and friends and a faith that in America, no one is left out; no one is left behind.

Let it be our cause that when she is able, she gives something back to her children, her community, and her country. And let it be our cause to give her a country that's coming together, and moving ahead – a country of boundless hopes and endless dreams; a country that once again lifts up its people, and inspires the world.

Let that be our cause and our commitment and our New Covenant.

I end tonight where it all began for me: I still believe in a place called Hope.

Nomination acceptance speech at the Democratic National Convention, 29 August 1996

President Bill Clinton accepted his nomination at the Democratic National Convention, 29 August 1996.

Possibly one of Clinton's finest speeches, it is long and well constructed with clever use of metaphor in reference to bridge building to the future and walking over that bridge together arm in arm. It sits well in the Clinton 5–7 status channel and uses emotional status to great effect pushing all the right buttons and actually stirring the crowd to respond vocally on a number of occasions. Brilliant management of audience focus.

Mr Chairman, Mr Vice President, my fellow Democrats, and my fellow Americans, thank you for your nomination. I don't know if I can find a fancy way to say this, but I accept.

Thank you.

So many – so many have contributed to the record we have made for the American people, but one above all: My partner, my friend, and the best vice president in our history – Al Gore.

Tonight – tonight, I thank the city of Chicago, its great mayor and its wonderful people for this magnificent convention. I love Chicago for many reasons – for your powerful spirit, your sports teams, your lively politics, but most of all for the love and light of my life – Chicago's daughter, Hillary. I love you.

You and I set forth on a journey to bring our vision to our country, to keep the American dream alive for all who are willing to work for it, to make our American community stronger, to keep America the world's strongest force for peace and freedom and prosperity.

Four years ago, with high unemployment, stagnant wages, crime, welfare and the deficit on the rise, with a host of unmet challenges and a rising tide of cynicism, I told you about a place I was born, and I told you I still believed in a place called Hope.

Well, for four years now, to realize our vision, we have pursued a simple but profound strategy – opportunity for all, responsibility from all, a strong united American community.

Four days ago as you were making your way here, I began a train ride to make my way to Chicago through America's heartland. I wanted to see the faces, I wanted to hear the voices of the people for whom I have worked and fought these last four years. And did I ever see them.

I met an ingenious businesswoman who was once on welfare in West Virginia; a brave police officer shot and paralyzed, now a civic leader in Kentucky. An auto worker in Ohio, once unemployed, now proud to be working in the oldest auto plant in America to help make America number one in auto production again for the first time in 20 years. I met a grandmother fighting for her grandson's environment in Michigan. And I stood with two wonderful little children proudly reading from their favorite book, 'The Little Engine That Could.'

At every stop large and exuberant crowds greeted me and, maybe more important, when we just rolled through little towns there were always schoolchildren there waving their American flags, all of them believing in America and its future.

I would not have missed that trip for all the world. For that trip showed me that hope is back in America. We are on the right track to the 21st century.

Look at the facts. Just look at the facts: 4.4 million Americans now living in a home of their own for the first time. Hundreds of thousands of women have started their own new businesses. More minorities own businesses than ever before. Record numbers of new small businesses and exports. Look at what's happened. We have the lowest combined rates of unemployment, inflation and home mortgages in 28 years.

Look at what happened. Ten million new jobs, over half of them high-wage jobs. Ten million workers getting the raise they deserve with the minimum wage law. Twenty-five million people now having protection in their health insurance because the Kennedy-Kassebaum bill says you can't lose your insurance anymore when you change jobs even if somebody in your family's been sick.

Forty million Americans with more pension security, a tax cut for 15 million of our hardest working, hardest pressed Americans and all small businesses. Twelve million Americans – 12 million of them taking advantage of the Family and Medical Leave Law so they could be good parents and good workers.

Ten million students have saved money on their college loans. We are making our democracy work. We have also passed political reform, the line-item veto bill, the motor voter bill, tougher registration laws for lobbyists, making Congress live under the laws they impose on the private sector, stopping unfunded mandates to state and local government. We've come a long way. We've got one more thing to do. Will you help me get campaign finance reform in the next four years?

We have increased our investments in research and technology. We have increased investments in breast cancer research dramatically. We are developing a supercomputer, a supercomputer that will do more calculating in a second than a person with a hand-held calculator can do in 30,000 years. More rapid development of drugs to deal with HIV and AIDS and moving them to the market quicker have almost doubled life expectancy in only four years, and we are looking at no limit in sight to that. We'll keep going until normal life is returned to people who deal with this.

Our country is still the strongest force for peace and freedom on earth. On issues that once before tore us apart, we have changed the old politics of Washington. For too long, leaders in Washington asked, 'Who's to blame?' But we asked, 'What are we going to do?'

On crime, we're putting 100,000 police on the streets. We made three-strikes-and-you're-out the law of the land. We stopped 60,000 felons, fugitives and stalkers from getting handguns under the Brady Bill. We banned assault rifles. We supported tougher punishment and prevention programs to keep our children from drugs and gangs and violence. Four years now – for four years now, the crime rate in America has gone down.

On welfare, we worked with states to launch a quiet revolution. Today, there are 1.8 million fewer people on welfare than there were the day I took the oath of office. We are moving people from welfare to work. We have increased child support collections by 40 percent. The federal workforce is the smallest it's been since John Kennedy. And the deficit has come down for four years in a row for the first time since before the Civil War – down 60 percent, on the way to zero. We will do it.

We are on the right track to the 21st century. We are on the right track, but our work is not finished. What should we do? First, let us consider how to proceed. Again, I say the question is no longer, 'Who's to blame?' but 'What to do?'

I believe that Bob Dole and Jack Kemp and Ross Perot love our country. And they have worked hard to serve it. It is legitimate, even necessary, to compare our record with theirs, our proposals for the future with theirs. And I expect them to make a vigorous effort to do the same. But I will not attack. I will not attack them personally, or permit others to do it in this party if I can prevent it.

My fellow Americans, this must be a campaign of ideas, not a campaign of insults. The American people deserve it. Now, here's the main idea. I love and revere the rich and proud history of America. And I am determined to take our best traditions into the future. But with all respect, we do not need to build a bridge to the past. We need to build a bridge to the future. And that is what I commit to you to do.

So tonight, let us resolve to build that bridge to the 21st century, to meet our challenges and protect our values. Let us build a bridge to help our parents raise their children, to help young people and adults to get the education and training they need, to make our streets safer, to help Americans succeed at home and at work, to break the cycle of poverty and dependence, to protect our environment for generations to come, and to maintain our world leadership for peace and freedom. Let us resolve to build that bridge.

Tonight, my fellow Americans, I ask all of our fellow citizens to join me and to join you in building that bridge to the 21st century.

Four years now – from now – just four years from now – think of it. We begin a new century full of enormous possibilities. We have to give the American people the tools they need to make the most of their God-given potential. We must make the basic bargain of opportunity and responsibility available to all Americans, not just a few. That is the promise of the Democratic Party, that is the promise of America.

I want to build a bridge to the 21st century in which we expand opportunity through education. Where computers are as much a part of the classroom as blackboards. Where highly trained teachers demand peak performance from their students. Where every eight-year-old can point to a book and say I can read it myself.

By the year 2000 the single most critical thing we can do is to give every single American who wants it the chance to go to college. We must make two years of college just as universal in four years as a high school education is today. And we can do it. We can do it and we should cut taxes to do it.

I propose a $1,500 a year tuition tax credit for Americans, a Hope Scholarship for the first two years of college to make the typical community college education available to every American. I believe every working family ought also to be able to deduct up to $10,000 in college tuition costs per year for education after that.

I believe the families of this country ought to be able to save money for college in a tax-free IRA, save it year in and year out withdraw it for a college education without penalty. We should not tax middle income Americans for the money they spend on college. We'll get the money back down the road many times over.

I want to say here before I go further that these tax cuts and every other one I mention tonight are all fully paid for in my balanced budget plan, line by line, dime by dime and they focus on education.

Now, one thing so many of our fellow Americans are learning is that education no longer stops on graduation day. I have proposed a new GI Bill for American workers – a $2,600 grant for unemployed and underemployed Americans so that they can get the training and the skills they need to go back to work at better-paying jobs, good high-skill jobs for a good future.

But we must demand excellence at every level of education. We must insist that our students learn the old basics we learned and the new basics they have to know for the next century. Tonight let us set a clear national goal. All children should be able to read on their own by the third grade.

When 40 percent of our eight-year-olds cannot read as well as they should, we have to do something. I want to send 30,000 reading specialists and National Service Corps members to mobilize a volunteer army of one million reading tutors for third graders all across America.

They will teach our young children to read. Let me say to our parents: You have to lead the way. Every tired night you spend reading a book to your child will be worth it many times over. I know that Hillary and I still talk about the books we read to Chelsea when we were so tired we could hardly stay awake. We still remember them. And, more important, so does she.

But we're going to help the parents of this country make every child able to read for himself or herself by the age of eight, by the third grade. Do you believe we can do that? Will you help us do that?

We must give parents, all parents, the right to choose which public school their children will attend and to let teachers form new charter schools with a charter they can keep only if they do a good job. We must keep our schools open late so that young people have some place to go and something to say yes to and stay off the street. We must require that our students pass tough tests to keep moving up in school. A diploma has to mean something when they get out.

We should reward teachers that are doing a good job, remove those who don't measure up. But, in every case, never forget that none of us would be here tonight if it weren't for our teachers. I know I wouldn't. We ought to lift them up, not tear them down.

We need schools that will take our children into the next century. We need schools that are rebuilt and modernized with an unprecedented commitment from the national government to increase school construction, and with every single library and classroom in America connected to the information superhighway by the year 2000.

Now folks, if we do these things, every eight-year-old will be able to read, every 12-year-old will be able to log in on the Internet, every 18-year-old will be able to go to college and all Americans will have the knowledge they need to cross that bridge to the 21st century.

I want to build a bridge to the 21st century in which we create a strong and growing economy to preserve the legacy of opportunity for the next generation by balancing our budget in a way that protects our values and ensuring that every family will be able to own and protect the value of their most important asset, their home.

Tonight, let us proclaim to the American people we will balance the budget, and let us also proclaim we will do it in a way that preserves Medicare, Medicaid, education, the environment, the integrity of our pensions, the strength of our people.

Now, last year – last year when the Republican Congress sent me a budget that violated those values and principles, I vetoed it, and I would do it again tomorrow. I could never allow cuts that devastate education for our children, that pollute our environment, that end the guarantee of health care for those who are served under Medicaid, that end our duty or violate our duty to our parents through Medicare. I just couldn't do that. As long as I'm president, I'll never let it happen.

And it doesn't matter – it doesn't matter if they try again, as they did before, to use the blackmail threat of a shutdown of the federal government to force these things on the American people. We didn't let it happen before. We won't let it happen again.

Of course, there is a better answer to this dilemma. We could have the right kind of balanced budget with a new Congress. A Democratic Congress.

I want to balance the budget with real cuts in government and waste. I want a plan that invests in education as mine does, in technology and yes, in research – as Christopher Reeve so powerfully reminded us we must do.

And my plan gives Americans tax cuts that will help our economy to grow. I want to expand IRAs so that young people can save tax free to buy a first home. Tonight I propose a new tax cut for home ownership that says to every middle income working family in this country, if you sell your home you will not have to pay a capital gains tax on it ever, not ever. I want every American to be able to hear those beautiful words: Welcome Home.

Let me say again. Every tax cut I call for tonight is targeted, it's responsible and it is paid for within my balanced budget plan. My tax cuts will not undermine our economy. They will speed economic growth. We should cut taxes for the family sending a child to college, for the worker returning to college, for the family saving to buy a home or for long term health care and a $500 per child credit for middle income families raising their children who need help with child care and what the children will do after school. That is the right way to cut taxes: Pro-family, pro-education, pro-economic growth.

Now, our opponents have put forward a very different plan – a risky $550 billion tax scheme that will force them to ask for even bigger cuts in Medicare, Medicaid, education and the environment than they passed and I vetoed last year.

But even then, they will not cover the cost of their scheme. So that even then this plan will explode the deficit, which will increase interest rates – by two percent according to their own estimates last year. It will require huge cuts in the very investments we need to grow and to grow together, and at the same time, slow down the economy. You know what higher interest rates mean. To you it means a higher mortgage payment, a higher car payment, a higher credit card payment. To our economy it means businesspeople will not borrow as much money, invest as much money, create as many new jobs, create as much wealth, raise as many raises.

Do we really want to make that same mistake all over again?

CROWD: No.

CLINTON: Do we really want to stop economic growth again?

CROWD: No.

CLINTON: Do we really want to start piling up another mountain of debt?

CROWD: No.

CLINTON: Do we want to bring back the recession of 1991 and '92?

CROWD: No.

CLINTON: Do we want to weaken our bridge to the 21st century?

CROWD: No.

CLINTON: Of course, we don't. We have an obligation, you and I, to leave our children a legacy of opportunity, not a legacy of debt. Our budget would be balanced today – we would have a surplus today – if we didn't have to make the interest payments on the debt run up in the 12 years before the Clinton–Gore administration took office. Thank you.

This is one of those areas in which I respectfully disagree with my opponent.

I don't believe we should bet the farm, and I certainly don't believe we should bet the country. We should stay on the right track to the 21st century. Opportunity alone is not enough. I want to build an America in the 21st century in which all Americans take personal responsibility for themselves, their families, their communities and their country.

I want our nation to take responsibility to make sure that every single child can look out the window in the morning and see a whole community getting up and going to work. We want these young people to know the thrill of the first paycheck, the challenge of starting that first business, the pride in following in a parent's footsteps.

The welfare reform law I signed last week gives America a chance, but not a guarantee, to have that kind of new beginning. To have a new social bargain with the poor, guaranteeing health care, child care and nutrition for the children, but requiring able-bodied parents to work for the income.

Now I say to all of you, whether you supported the law or opposed it – but especially to those who supported it – we have a responsibility, we have a moral obligation to make sure the people who are being required to work have the opportunity to work. We must make sure the jobs are there.

There should be one million new jobs for welfare recipients by the year 2000. States under this law can now take the money that was spent on the welfare check and use it to help businesses provide paychecks. I challenge every state to do it soon. I propose also to give businesses a tax credit for every person hired off welfare and kept employed.

I propose to offer private job placement firms a bonus for every welfare recipient they place in a job who stays in it. And, more important, I want to help communities put welfare recipients to work right now, without delay, repairing schools, making their neighborhoods clean and safe, making them shine again. There's lots of work to be done out there. Our cities can find ways to put people to work and bring dignity and strength back to these families.

My fellow Americans, I have spent an enormous amount of time, with our dear friend, the late Ron Brown, and with Secretary Kantor and others, opening markets for America around the world. And I'm proud of every one we opened. But let us never forget the greatest untapped market for American enterprise is right here in America, in the inner cities, in the rural areas, who have not felt this recovery.

With investment and business and jobs they can become our partners in the future. And it's a great opportunity we ought not to pass up. I propose more empowerment zones, like the one we have right here in Chicago to draw business into poor neighborhoods.

I propose more community development banks, like the Southshore Bank right here in Chicago to help people in those neighborhoods start their own small businesses – more jobs, more incomes, new markets for America, right here at home making welfare reform a reality.

Now, folks, you cheered and I thank you. But the government can only do so much. The private sector has to provide most of these jobs. So I want to say again, tonight I challenge every business person in America who has ever complained about the failure of the welfare system to try to hire somebody off welfare. And try hard.

Thank you. After all, the welfare system you used to complain about is not here anymore. There is no more 'who's to blame?' on welfare. Now the only question is what to do. And we all have a responsibility, especially those who have criticized what was passed and who have asked for a change and who have the ability to give the poor a chance to grow and support their families.

I want to build a bridge to the 21st century that ends the permanent underclass, that lifts up the poor and ends their isolation, their exile, and they are not forgotten anymore.

I want to build a bridge to the 21st century where our children are not killing other children any more. Where children's lives are not shattered by violence at home or in the schoolyard. Where a generation of young people are not left to raise themselves on the streets. With more police and punishment and prevention the crime rate has dropped for four years in a row, now. But we cannot rest, because we know it's still too high. We cannot rest until crime is a shocking exception to our daily lives, not news as usual. Will you stay with me until we reach that good day?

CROWD: Yes!

My fellow Americans, we all owe a great debt to Sarah and Jim Brady and I'm glad they took their wrong turn and wound up in Chicago. I was glad to see them. It is to them we owe the good news that 60,000 felons, fugitives and stalkers couldn't get hand guns because of the Brady bill. But not a single hunter in Arkansas or New Hampshire or Illinois or anyplace else missed a hunting season.

But now I say we should extend the Brady bill because anyone who has committed an act of domestic violence against a spouse or a child should not buy a gun. And we must ban – we must ban those cop-killer bullets. They are designed for one reason only – to kill police officers.

We ask the police to keep us safe. We owe it to them to help keep them safe while they do their job for us. We should pass a victims' rights constitutional amendment because victims deserve to be heard. They need to know when an assailant is released. They need to know these things, and the only way to guarantee them is through a constitutional amendment.

We have made a great deal of progress. Even the crime rate among young people is finally coming down. So it is very, very painful to me that drug use among young people is up. Drugs nearly killed my brother when he was a young man and I hate them.

He fought back. He's here tonight with his wife. His little boy is here. And I'm really proud of him. But I learned something in going through that long nightmare with our family. And I can tell you, something has happened to some of our young people. They simply don't think these drugs are dangerous anymore. Or they think the risk is acceptable.

So beginning with our parents and without regard to our party, we have to renew our energy to teach this generation of young people the hard, cold truth.

Drugs are deadly. Drugs are wrong. Drugs can cost you your life. General Barry McCaffrey, the four-star general who led our fight against drugs in Latin America, now leads our crusade against drugs at home – stopping more drugs at our borders, cracking down on those who sell them, and most important of all, pursuing a national anti-drug strategy whose primary aim is to turn our children away from drugs. I call on Congress to give him every cent of funding we have requested for this strategy and to do it now.

There is more we will do. We should say to parolees, we will test you for drugs. If you go back on them, we will send you back to jail. We will say to gangs, we will break with the same anti-racketeering law we used to put mob bosses in jail. You're not going to kill our kids anymore or turn them into murderers before they're teenagers.

My fellow Americans, if we're going to build that bridge to the 21st century, we have to make our children free – free of the vise grip of guns and gangs and drugs; free to build lives of hope.

I want to build a bridge to the 21st century with a strong American community beginning with strong families. An America where all children are cherished and protected from destructive forces, where parents can succeed at home and at work. Everywhere I've gone in America, people come up and talk to me about their struggle with the demands of work and their desire to do a better job with their children. The very first person I ever saw fight that battle was here with me four years ago. And tonight, I miss her very, very much. My irrepressible, hardworking, always optimistic mother did the best she could for her brother and me, often against very stiff odds.

I learned from her just how much love and determination can overcome. But from her and from our life, I also learned that no parent can do it alone. And no parent should have to. She had the kind of help every parent deserves from our neighbors, our friends, our teachers, our pastors, our doctors and so many more.

You know, when I started out in public life with a lot of my friends from the Arkansas delegation down here there used to be a saying we'd hear from time to time, that every man who runs for public office will claim that he was born in a log cabin he built with his own hands. Well, my mother knew better. And she made sure I did too. Long before she even met Hillary my mother knew it takes a village. And she was grateful for the support she got.

As Tipper Gore and Hillary said on Tuesday, we have, all of us in our administration, worked hard to support families in raising their children and succeeding at work. But we must do more. We should extend the Family and Medical Leave Law to give parents some time off to take their children to regular doctors appointments or attend those parent-teacher Conferences at school. That is a key determination of their success.

We should pass a flex-time law that allows employees to take their overtime pay in money, or in time off, depending on what's better for their family.

The FDA has adopted new measures to reduce advertising and sales of cigarettes to children. The vice president spoke so movingly of it last night.

But let me remind you, my fellow Americans, that is very much an issue in this election, because that battle is far from over and the two candidates have different views. I pledge to America's parents that I will see this effort all the way through.

Working with the entertainment industry, we're giving parents the V-chip. TV shows are being rated for content so parents will be able to make a judgment about whether their small children should see them. And three hours of quality children's programming every week on every network are on the way.

The Kennedy–Kassebaum law says every American can keep his or her health insurance if they have to change jobs, even if someone in their family's been sick. That is a very important thing. But tonight, we should spell out the next steps.

The first thing we ought to do is to extend the benefits of health care to people who are unemployed. I propose in my balanced budget plan, paid for, to help unemployed families keep their health insurance for up to six months.

A parent may be without a job, but no child should be without a doctor. And let me say again as the first lady did on Tuesday, we should protect mothers and newborn babies from being forced out of the hospital in less than 48 hours.

We respect the individual conscience of every American on the painful issue of abortion, but believe as a matter of law that this decision should be left to a woman, her conscience, her doctor and her God.

But abortion should not only be safe and legal, it should be rare. That's why I helped to establish and support a national effort to reduce out-of-wedlock teen pregnancy, and that is why we must promote adoption.

Last week, the minimum wage bill I signed contained a $5,000 credit to families who adopt children – even more, if the children have disabilities. It put an end to racial discrimination in the adoption process. It was a good thing for America.

My fellow Americans, already there are tens of thousands of children out there who need a good home with loving parents. I hope more of them will find it now.

I want to build a bridge to the 21st century with a clean and safe environment. We are making our food safer from pesticides. We're protecting our drinking water and our air from poisons. We saved Yellowstone from mining. We established the largest national park south of Alaska in the Mojave Desert in California. We are working to save the precious Florida Everglades. And when the leaders of this Congress invited the polluters into the back room to roll back 25 years of environmental protections that both parties had always supported I said no.

But we must do more.

Today 10 million children live within just four miles of a toxic waste dump. We've cleaned up 197 of those dumps in the last three years, more than in the previous 12 years combined. In the next four years, we propose to clean up 500 more – two-thirds of all that are left and the most dangerous ones. Our children should grow up next to parks, not poison.

We should make it a crime even to attempt to pollute. We should freeze the serious polluter's property until they clean up the problems they create. We should make it easier so they can do more to protect their own children. These are the things that we must do to build that bridge to the 21st century.

My fellow Americans, I want to build a bridge to the 21st century that makes sure we are still the nation with the world's strongest defense, that our foreign policy still advances the values of our American community in the community of nations.

Our bridge to the future must include bridges to other nations, because we remain the world's indispensable nation to advance prosperity, peace and freedom and to keep our own children safe from the dangers of terror and weapons of mass destruction.

We have helped to bring democracy to Haiti and peace to Bosnia. Now, the peace signed on the White House lawn between the Israelis and the Palestinians must embrace more of Israel's neighbors.

The deep desire for peace that Hillary and I felt when we walked the streets of Belfast and Derry must become real for all the people of Northern Ireland, and Cuba must finally join the community of democracies.

Nothing in our lifetimes has been more heartening than when people of the former Soviet Union and Central Europe broke the grip of communism. We have aided their progress and I am proud of it. And I will continue our strong partnership with a democratic Russia.

And we will bring some of Central Europe's new democracies into NATO so that they will never question their own freedom in the future.

Our American exports are at record levels. In the next four years, we have to break down even more barriers to them, reaching out to Latin America, to Africa, to other countries in Asia, making sure that our workers and our products – the world's finest – have the benefit of free and fair trade.

In the last four years, we have frozen North Korea's nuclear weapons program. And I'm proud to say that tonight there is not a single Russian nuclear missile pointed at an American child.

Now, now we must enforce and ratify without delay measures that further reduce nuclear arsenals, banish poison gas and ban nuclear tests once and for all. We have made investments, new investments in our most important defense asset: Our magnificent men and women in uniform.

By the year 2000 we also will have increased funding to modernize our weapons systems by 40 percent. These commitments will make sure that our military remains the best trained, best equipped fighting force in the entire world.

We are developing a sensible national missile defense, but we must not, not now, not by the year 2000, squander $60 billion on an unproved, ineffective Star Wars program that could be obsolete tomorrow.

We are fighting terrorism on all fronts with a three-pronged strategy. First, we are working to rally a world coalition with zero-tolerance for terrorism. Just this month I signed a law imposing harsh sanctions on foreign companies that invest in key sectors of the Iranian and Libyan economies.

As long as Iran trains, supports and protects terrorists, as long as Libya refuses to give up the people who blew up Pan Am 103, they will pay a price from the United States.

Second, we must give law endorsement the tools they need to take the fight to terrorists. We need new laws to crack down on money laundering and to prosecute and punish those who commit violent acts against American citizens abroad; to add chemical markers or taggants to gunpowder used in bombs so we can track the bombmakers.

To extend the same power police now have against organized crime to save lives by tapping all the phones that terrorists use. Terrorists are as big a threat to our future, perhaps bigger, than organized crime. Why should we have two different standards for a common threat to the safety of America and our children?

We need, in short, the laws that Congress refused to pass. And I ask them again – please, as an American, not a partisan, matter, pass these laws now.

Third, we will improve airport and air travel security. I have asked the vice president to establish a commission and report back to me on ways to do this. But now we will install the most sophisticated bomb detection equipment in all our major airports. We will search every airplane flying to or from America from another nation – every flight, every cargo hold, every cabin, every time.

My fellow Democrats and my fellow Americans, I know that in most election seasons, foreign policy is not a matter of great interest in the debates in the barbershops and the cafes of America, on the plant floors and at the bowling alleys. But there are times – there are times when only America can make the difference between war and peace, between freedom and repression, between life and death.

We cannot save all the world's children, but we can save many of them. We cannot become the world's policeman, but where our values and our interests are at stake, and where we can make a difference, we must act and we must lead. That is our job and we are better, stronger and safer because we are doing it.

My fellow Americans, let me say one last time. We can only build our bridge to the 21st century if we build it together, and if we're willing to walk arm-in-arm across that bridge together.

I have spent so much of your time that you gave me these last four years to be your president worrying about the problems of Bosnia, the Middle East, Northern Ireland, Rwanda, Burundi. What do these places have in common?

People are killing each other and butchering children because they are different from one another. They share the same piece of land, but they are different from one another. They hate their race, their tribe, their ethnic group, their religion. We have seen the terrible, terrible price that people pay when they insist on fighting and killing their neighbors over their differences.

In our own country, we have seen America pay a terrible price for any form of discrimination. And we have seen us grow stronger as we have steadily let more and more of our hatreds and our fears go, as we have given more and more of our people the chance to live their dreams.

That is why the flame of our Statue of Liberty, like the Olympic flame carried all across America by thousands of citizen heroes, will always, always burn brighter than the fires that burn our churches, our synagogues, our mosques, always.

Look around this hall tonight. And there are fellow Americans watching on television. You look around this hall tonight. There is every conceivable difference here among the people who are gathered.

If we want to build that bridge to the 21st century, we have to be willing to say loud and clear: If you believe in the values of the Constitution, the Bill of Rights, the Declaration of Independence, if you're willing to work hard and play by the rules, you are part of our family. And we're proud to be with you.

You cheer now because you know this is true. You know this is true. When you walk out of this hall, think about it. Live by it.

We still have too many Americans who give in to their fears of those who are different from them. Not so long ago, swastikas were painted on the doors of some African-American members of our Special Forces at Ft. Bragg.

Folks, for those of you who don't know what they do, the Special Forces are just what the name says. They are special forces. If I walk off this stage tonight and call them on the telephone and tell them to go halfway around the world and risk their lives for you and be there by tomorrow at noon, they will do it. They do not deserve to have swastikas on their doors.

CROWD: Four more years! Four more years! Four more years! Four more years!

Look around here. Old or young, healthy as a horse or a person with a disability that hadn't kept you down, man or woman, Native American, native born, immigrant, straight or gay – whatever the test ought to be I believe in the Constitution, the Bill of Rights, and the Declaration of Independence.

I believe in religious liberty. I believe in freedom of speech. I believe in working hard and playing by the rules. I'm showing up for work tomorrow. I'm building that bridge to the 21st century.

That ought to be the test.

My fellow Americans 68 nights from tonight the American people will face once again a critical moment of decision. We're going to choose the last president of the 20th century and the first president of the 21st century.

But the real choice is not that. The real choice is whether we will build a bridge to the future or a bridge to the past; about whether we believe our best days are still out there or our best days are behind us; about whether we want a country of people all working together, or one where you're on your own.

Let us commit ourselves this night to rise up and build the bridge we know we ought to build all the way to the 21st century.

And let us have faith, faith, American faith, American faith that we are not leaving our greatness behind. We're going to carry it right on with us into that new century. A century of new challenge and unlimited promise.

Let us, in short, do the work that is before us, so that when our time here is over we will all watch the sun go down as we all must, and say truly, we have prepared our children for the dawn.

My fellow Americans, after these four good, hard years I still believe in the place called Hope – a place called America. Thank you. God bless you. And good night.

Speech at the annual White House prayer breakfast, 11 September 1998

Clinton gave this speech at the annual White House prayer breakfast on 11 September 1998. The audience was made up of more than a 100 religious leaders and his wife Hillary.

Probably the most difficult and one of the shortest speeches of his Presidency. It is low key – definitely at the 5 end of the 5–7 status channel and a great demonstration in focus of how to use first and third circles of concentration and indeed first in third.

'I Have Sinned'

Thank you very much, ladies and gentlemen. Welcome to the White House and to this day to which Hillary and the vice president and I look forward so much every year.

This is always an important day for our country, for the reasons that the vice president said. It is an unusual and, I think, unusually important day today. I may not be quite as easy with my words today as I have been in years past, and I was up rather late last night thinking about and praying about what I ought to say today. And rather unusual for me, I actually tried to write it down. So if you will forgive me, I will do my best to say what it is I want to say to you – and I may have to take my glasses out to read my own writing.

First, I want to say to all of you that, as you might imagine, I have been on quite a journey these last few weeks to get to the end of this, to the rock bottom truth of where I am and where we all are.

I agree with those who have said that in my first statement after I testified I was not contrite enough. I don't think there is a fancy way to say that I have sinned.

It is important to me that everybody who has been hurt know that the sorrow I feel is genuine: first and most important, my family; also my friends, my staff, my Cabinet, Monica Lewinsky and her family, and the American people. I have asked all for their forgiveness.

But I believe that to be forgiven, more than sorrow is required – at least two more things. First, genuine repentance – a determination to change and to repair breaches of my own making. I have repented. Second, what my bible calls a 'broken spirit'; an understanding that I must have God's help to be the person that I want to be; a willingness to give the very forgiveness I seek; a renunciation of the pride and the anger which cloud judgment, lead people to excuse and compare and to blame and complain.

Now, what does all this mean for me and for us? First, I will instruct my lawyers to mount a vigorous defence, using all available appropriate arguments. But legal language must not obscure the fact that I have done wrong. Second, I will continue on the path of repentance, seeking pastoral support and that of other caring people so that they can hold me accountable for my own commitment.

Third, I will intensify my efforts to lead our country and the world toward peace and freedom, prosperity and harmony, in the hope that with a broken spirit and a still strong heart I can be used for greater good, for we have many blessings and many challenges and so much work to do.

In this, I ask for your prayers and for your help in healing our nation. And though I cannot move beyond or forget this – indeed, I must always keep it as a caution light in my life – it is very important that our nation move forward.

I am very grateful for the many, many people – clergy and ordinary citizens alike – who have written me with wise counsel. I am profoundly grateful for the support of so many Americans who somehow through it all seem to still know that I care about them a great deal, that I care about their problems and their dreams. I am grateful for those who have stood by me and who say that in this case and many others, the bounds of privacy have been excessively and unwisely invaded. That may be. Nevertheless, in this case, it may be a blessing, because I still sinned. And if my repentance is genuine and sustained, and if I can maintain both a broken spirit and a strong heart, then good can come of this for our country as well as for me and my family.

The children of this country can learn in a profound way that integrity is important and selfishness is wrong, but God can change us and make us strong at the broken places. I want to embody those lessons for the children of this country – for that little boy in Florida who came up to me and said that he wanted to grow up and be President and to be just like me. I want the parents of all the children in America to be able to say that to their children.

A couple of days ago when I was in Florida a Jewish friend of mine gave me this liturgy book called 'Gates of Repentance.' And there was this incredible passage from the Yom Kippur liturgy. I would like to read it to you:

> 'Now is the time for turning. The leaves are beginning to turn from green to red to orange. The birds are beginning to turn and are heading once more toward the south. The animals are beginning to turn to storing their food for the winter. For leaves, birds and animals, turning comes instinctively. But for us, turning does not come so easily. It takes an act of will for us to make a turn. It means breaking old habits. It means admitting that we have been wrong, and this is never easy. It means losing face. It means starting all over again. And this is always painful. It means saying I am sorry. It means recognizing that we have the ability to change. These things are terribly hard to do. But unless we turn, we will be trapped forever in yesterday's ways. Lord help us to turn, from callousness to sensitivity, from hostility to love, from pettiness to purpose, from envy to contentment, from carelessness to discipline, from fear to faith. Turn us around, O Lord, and bring us back toward you. Revive our lives as at the beginning, and turn us toward each other, Lord, for in isolation there is no life.'

I thank my friend for that. I thank you for being here. I ask you to share my prayer that God will search me and know my heart, try me and know my anxious thoughts, see if there is any hurtfulness in me, and lead me toward the life everlasting. I ask that God give me a clean heart, let me walk by faith and not sight.

I ask once again to be able to love my neighbor – all my neighbors – as myself, to be an instrument of God's peace; to let the words of my mouth and the meditations of my heart and, in the end, the work of my hands, be pleasing. This is what I wanted to say to you today.

Thank you. God bless you.

Nation Farewell Speech, 18 January 2001

This was the speech President Clinton gave in his Nation Farewell on 18 January 2001

A short, well balanced and cleverly crafted speech in which Bill Clinton does what he does best – share himself with his audience. Perfect status level and great use of first circle of concentration bringing the 3 Rs of recall, reflection and reason into play. He also uses first circle as a springboard to second making sure that everyone watching would feel personally addressed.

My fellow citizens, tonight is my last opportunity to speak to you from the Oval Office as your President. I am profoundly grateful to you for twice giving me the honor to serve – to work for you and with you to prepare our nation for the 21st century.

And I'm grateful to Vice President Gore, to my Cabinet Secretaries, and to all those who have served with me for the last eight years.

This has been a time of dramatic transformation, and you have risen to every new challenge. You have made our social fabric stronger, our families healthier and safer, our people more prosperous. You, the American people, have made our passage into the global information age an era of great American renewal.

In all the work I have done as President – every decision I have made, every executive action I have taken, every bill I have proposed and signed, I've tried to give all Americans the tools and conditions to build the future of our dreams in a good society, with a strong economy, a cleaner environment, and a freer, safer, more prosperous world.

I have steered my course by our enduring values – opportunity for all, responsibility from all, a community of all Americans. I have sought to give America a new kind of government, smaller, more modern, more effective, full of ideas and policies appropriate to this new time, always putting people first, always focusing on the future.

Working together, America has done well. Our economy is breaking records, with more than 22 million new jobs, the lowest unemployment in 30 years, the highest home ownership ever, the longest expansion in history.

Our families and communities are stronger. Thirty-five million Americans have used the Family Leave law; 8 million have moved off welfare. Crime is at a 25-year low. Over 10 million Americans receive more college aid, and more people than ever are going to college. Our schools are better. Higher standards, greater accountability and larger investments have brought higher test scores and higher graduation rates.

More than 3 million children have health insurance now, and more than 7 million Americans have been lifted out of poverty. Incomes are rising across the board. Our air and water are cleaner. Our food and drinking water are safer. And more of our precious land has been preserved in the continental United States than at any time in a hundred years.

America has been a force for peace and prosperity in every corner of the globe. I'm very grateful to be able to turn over the reins of leadership to a new President with America in such a strong position to meet the challenges of the future.

Tonight I want to leave you with three thoughts about our future. First, America must maintain our record of fiscal responsibility.

Through our last four budgets we've turned record deficits to record surpluses, and we've been able to pay down $600 billion of our national debt, on track to be debt-free by the end of the decade for the first time since 1835. Staying on that course will bring lower interest rates, greater prosperity, and the opportunity to meet our big challenges. If we choose wisely, we can pay down the debt, deal with the retirement of the baby boomers, invest more in our future, and provide tax relief.

Second, because the world is more connected every day, in every way, America's security and prosperity require us to continue to lead in the world. At this remarkable moment in history, more people live in freedom than ever before. Our alliances are stronger than ever. People all around the world look to America to be a force for peace and prosperity, freedom and security.

The global economy is giving more of our own people and billions around the world the chance to work and live and raise their families with dignity. But the forces of integration that have created these good opportunities also make us more subject to global forces of destruction – to terrorism, organized crime and narco trafficking, the spread of deadly weapons and disease, the degradation of the global environment.

The expansion of trade hasn't fully closed the gap between those of us who live on the cutting edge of the global economy and the billions around the world who live on the knife's edge of survival. This global gap requires more than compassion; it requires action. Global poverty is a powder keg that could be ignited by our indifference.

In his first inaugural address, Thomas Jefferson warned of entangling alliances. But in our times, America cannot, and must not, disentangle itself from the world. If we want the world to embody our shared values, then we must assume a shared responsibility.

If the wars of the 20th century, especially the recent ones in Kosovo and Bosnia, have taught us anything, it is that we achieve our aims by defending our values, and leading the forces of freedom and peace. We must embrace boldly and resolutely that duty to lead – to stand with our allies in word and deed, and to put a human face on the global economy, so that expanded trade benefits all peoples in all nations, lifting lives and hopes all across the world.

Third, we must remember that America cannot lead in the world unless here at home we weave the threads of our coat of many colors into the fabric of one America. As we become ever more diverse, we must work harder to unite around our common values and our common humanity. We must work harder to overcome our differences, in our hearts and in our laws. We must treat all our people with fairness and dignity, regardless of their race, religion, gender or sexual orientation, and regardless of when they arrived in our country; always moving toward the more perfect union of our founders' dreams.

Hillary, Chelsea and I join all Americans in wishing our very best to the next President, George W. Bush, to his family and his administration, in meeting these challenges, and in leading freedom's march in this new century.

As for me, I'll leave the presidency more idealistic, more full of hope than the day I arrived, and more confident than ever that America's best days lie ahead.

My days in this office are nearly through, but my days of service, I hope, are not. In the years ahead, I will never hold a position higher or a covenant more sacred than that of President of the United States. But there is no title I will wear more proudly than that of citizen.

Thank you. God bless you, and God bless America.

'We shall fight on the beaches'

Winston Churchill gave this speech on 4 June 1940 to the House Of Commons. Although often known as 'We shall fight them on the beaches', this is in fact a misquotation of 'We shall fight on the beaches'.

Churchill's inspiring rhetoric preparing the nation for the struggle ahead marches indomitably forward with an almost hypnotic rhythm. It is this wonderful regular meter that is in part responsible for making the speech so memorable. It will, of course, always be remembered for the stirring repetition of 'we shall fight …' – the technique known as anaphora, whereby a word or phrase is emphasized by it being repeated at the beginning of successive clauses or sentences. There is also a tremendous feeling of strength in his lack of emotion. Perhaps this was a well chosen level of emotional status selected for the speech to achieve its crucial goal at the time.

Turning once again, and this time more generally, to the question of invasion, I would observe that there has never been a period in all these long centuries of which we boast when an absolute guarantee against invasion, still less against serious raids, could have been given to our people.

In the days of Napoleon the same wind which would have carried his transports across the Channel might have driven away the blockading fleet. There was always the chance, and it is that chance which has excited and befooled the imaginations of many Continental tyrants.

Many are the tales that are told. We are assured that novel methods will be adopted, and when we see the originality of malice, the ingenuity of aggression, which our enemy displays, we may certainly prepare ourselves for every kind of novel stratagem and every kind of brutal and treacherous manoeuvre. I think that no idea is so outlandish that it should not be considered and viewed with a searching, but at the same time, I hope, with a steady eye. We must never forget the solid assurances of sea power and those which belong to air power if it can be locally exercised.

I have, myself, full confidence that if all do their duty, if nothing is neglected, and if the best arrangements are made, as they are being made, we shall prove ourselves once again able to defend our Island home, to ride out the storm of war, and to outlive the menace of tyranny, if necessary for years, if necessary alone.

At any rate, that is what we are going to try to do. That is the resolve of His Majesty's Government – every man of them. That is the will of Parliament and the nation.

The British Empire and the French Republic, linked together in their cause and in their need, will defend to the death their native soil, aiding each other like good comrades to the utmost of their strength.

Even though large tracts of Europe and many old and famous States have fallen or may fall into the grip of the Gestapo and all the odious apparatus of Nazi rule, we shall not flag or fail.

We shall go on to the end, we shall fight in France,
we shall fight on the seas and oceans,
we shall fight with growing confidence and growing strength in the air,
we shall defend our Island, whatever the cost may be,
we shall fight on the beaches,
we shall fight on the landing grounds,
we shall fight in the fields and in the streets,
we shall fight in the hills;

we shall never surrender, and even if, which I do not for a moment believe, this Island or a large part of it were subjugated and starving, then our Empire beyond the seas, armed and guarded by the British Fleet, would carry on the struggle, until, in God's good time, the New World, with all its power and might, steps forth to the rescue and the liberation of the old.

'Ich bin ein Berliner'

President Kennedy gave this speech in Berlin on 26 June 1963. His audience was a crowd in the Rudolph Wilde Platz near the Berlin Wall.

An absolutely marvellous speech made to the people of West Berlin, it is an acknowledgement to their great spirit. Kennedy displays a wonderful management of personal focus using the circles of concentration very effectively, while his astute choice of mid-level status gave the people real access to him. There are echoes of Martin Luther King with his theme of freedom, and the repetition of 'let them come to Berlin!' really hits the spot with the locals! Great stuff!

I am proud to come to this city as the guest of your distinguished Mayor, who has symbolized throughout the world the fighting spirit of West Berlin. And I am proud to visit the Federal Republic with your distinguished Chancellor who for so many years has committed Germany to democracy and freedom and progress, and to come here in the company of my fellow American, General Clay, who has been in this city during its great moments of crisis and will come again if ever needed.

Two thousand years ago the proudest boast was '*civis Romanus sum*.' Today, in the world of freedom, the proudest boast is '*Ich bin ein Berliner*.'

I appreciate my interpreter translating my German!

There are many people in the world who really don't understand, or say they don't, what is the great issue between the free world and the Communist world. Let them come to Berlin. There are some who say that communism is the wave of the future. Let them come to Berlin. And there are some who say in Europe and elsewhere we can work with the Communists. Let them come to Berlin. And there are even a few who say that it is true that communism is an evil system, but it permits us to make economic progress. *Lass' sie nach Berlin kommen*. Let them come to Berlin.

Freedom has many difficulties and democracy is not perfect, but we have never had to put a wall up to keep our people in, to prevent them from leaving us. I want to say, on behalf of my countrymen, who live many miles away on the other side of the Atlantic, who are far distant from you, that they take the greatest pride that they have been able to share with you, even from a distance, the story of the last 18 years. I know of no town, no city, that has been besieged for 18 years that still lives with the vitality and the force, and the hope and the determination of the city of West Berlin. While the wall is the most obvious and vivid demonstration of the failures of the Communist system, for all the world to see, we take no satisfaction in it, for it is, as your Mayor has said, an offense not only against history but an offense against humanity, separating families, dividing husbands and wives and brothers and sisters, and dividing a people who wish to be joined together.

What is true of this city is true of Germany – real, lasting peace in Europe can never be assured as long as one German out of four is denied the elementary right of free men, and that is to make a free choice. In 18 years of peace and good faith, this generation of Germans has earned the right to be free, including the right to unite their families and their nation in lasting peace, with good will to all people. You live in a defended island of freedom, but your life is part of the main. So let me ask you as I close, to lift your eyes beyond the dangers of today, to the hopes of tomorrow, beyond the freedom merely of this city of Berlin, or your country of Germany, to the advance of freedom everywhere, beyond the wall to the day of peace with justice, beyond yourselves and ourselves to all mankind.

Freedom is indivisible, and when one man is enslaved, all are not free. When all are free, then we can look forward to that day when this city will be joined as one and this country and this great Continent of Europe in a peaceful and hopeful globe. When that day finally comes, as it will, the people of West Berlin can take sober satisfaction in the fact that they were in the front lines for almost two decades.

All free men, wherever they may live, are citizens of Berlin, and, therefore, as a free man, I take pride in the words, '*Ich bin ein Berliner.*'

'Magnanimous in victory'

This is the speech that Lieutenant Colonel Tim Collins gave the battlegroup of the 1st Battalion of the Royal Irish Regiment at the Mayne desert camp, 20 miles from the Iraqi border. The US deadline for Saddam Hussein to leave Iraq or face military action was fast approaching.

A truly stirring speech which left his men in absolutely no doubt of what was expected of them and of their duty to the Iraqi people. Delivered with the skill of a great performer dancing around in the 5–7 status channel and using all three circles of concentration for dramatic impact. A modern day classic. In March 2008 it was dramatized on BBC television, with Kenneth Branagh playing the role of Tim Collins.

We go to liberate, not to conquer.

We will not fly our flags in their country

We are entering Iraq to free a people and the only flag which will be flown in that ancient land is their own.

Show respect for them.

There are some who are alive at this moment who will not be alive shortly.

Those who do not wish to go on that journey, we will not send.

As for the others, I expect you to rock their world.

Wipe them out if that is what they choose.

But if you are ferocious in battle remember to be magnanimous in victory.

Iraq is steeped in history.

It is the site of the Garden of Eden, of the Great Flood and the birthplace of Abraham.

Tread lightly there.

You will see things that no man could pay to see – and you will have to go a long way to find a more decent, generous and upright people than the Iraqis. You will be embarrassed by their hospitality even though they have nothing.

Don't treat them as refugees for they are in their own country. Their children will be poor, in years to come they will know that the light of liberation in their lives was brought by you.

If there are casualties of war then remember that when they woke up and got dressed in the morning they did not plan to die this day. Allow them dignity in death. Bury them properly and mark their graves.

It is my foremost intention to bring every single one of you out alive. But there may be people among us who will not see the end of this campaign. We will put them in their sleeping bags and send them back. There will be no time for sorrow.

The enemy should be in no doubt that we are his nemesis and that we are bringing about his rightful destruction. There are many regional commanders who have stains on their souls and they are stoking the fires of hell for Saddam. He and his forces will be destroyed by this coalition for what they have done. As they die they will know their deeds have brought them to this place. Show them no pity.

It is a big step to take another human life. It is not to be done lightly. I know of men who have taken life needlessly in other conflicts. I can assure you they live with the mark of Cain upon them.

If someone surrenders to you then remember they have that right in international law and ensure that one day they go home to their family. The ones who wish to fight, well, we aim to please.

If you harm the regiment or its history by over-enthusiasm in killing or in cowardice, know it is your family who will suffer. You will be shunned unless your conduct is of the highest – for your deeds will follow you down through history. We will bring shame on neither our uniform nor our nation.

It is not a question of if, it's a question of when. We know he has already devolved the decision to lower commanders, and that means he has already taken the decision himself. If we survive the first strike we will survive the attack.

As for ourselves, let's bring everyone home and leave Iraq a better place for us having been there.

Our business now is North.

Bill Clinton

My Life by Bill Clinton

Boy Clinton – A Political Biography by R. Emmett Tyrell

First In His Class – A Biography Of Bill Clinton by David Maraniss

The Survivor – Bill Clinton in the White House by John F. Harris

A Woman in Charge – The Life of Hilary Rodham Clinton by Carl Bernstein

Story

Aesop's Fables

Fairy Tales by the Brothers Grimm

The Greek Myths by Robert Graves

The Art of Rhetoric by Aristotle

On the Ideal Orator by Cicero

Story (Substance, Structure, Style and the Principles of Screenwriting) by Robert McKee

Status and focus

Stanislavski and acting systems

An Actor Prepares by Konstantin Stanislavski

Creating a Role by Konstantin Stanislavski

My Life in Art by Konstantin Stanislavski

Building a Character by Konstantin Stanislavski

Acting – A Handbook of the Stanislavski Method by Toby Cole

A Dream of Passion – The Development of the Method by Lee Strasberg

Stella Adler – The Art of Acting by Stella Adler and Howard Kissel

To the Actor by Michael Chekhov

Stanislavski for Beginners by David Allen

The Stanislavski System – The Professional Training of an Actor by Sonia Moore

Emotional Intelligence by Daniel Goleman

Body Language by Geoff Ribbens and Greg Whitear

The Right to Speak – Working With the Voice by Patsy Rodenburg

On the Web

Bill Clinton

www.clintonfoundation.org
www.clintonlibrary.gov
www.whitehouse.gov/history/presidents/bc42
www.clintonpresidentialcenter.org

Hilary Clinton

www.clinton.senate.gov

Performance

www.strasberg.com (The Lee Strasberg Theatre and Film Institute New York and Los Angeles)

www.theactorsstudio.org (The Actors' Studio, New York)

http://www.pace.edu/ (The Actors Studio MFA in acting, directing and playwriting at Pace University, New York City)

Clinton's favourite books

In 2003, Bill Clinton released a list of his 21 favourite books to help publicise the Clinton Library and an exhibition of books and gifts he had received while President. This list gives us some insight into his literary tastes and his appreciation of story.

I Know Why the Caged Bird Sings by Maya Angelou

Meditation by Marcus Aureiius

The Denial of Death by Ernest Becker

Parting the Waters: America in the King Years 1954–1963 by Taylor Branch

Living History by Hillary Rodham Clinton

Lincoln by David Herbert Donald

The Four Quarters by T. S. Eliot

Invisible Man by Ralph Ellison

The Way of the World: From the Dawn of Civilizations to the Eve of the Twenty-First Century by David Fromkin

One Hundred Years of Solitude by Gabriel Garcia Marquez

The Cure at Troy: A Version of Sophocies' Philoctetes by Seamus Heaney

King Leopold's Ghost: A Story of Greed, Terror and Heroism and Colonial Africa by Adam Hochschild

The Imitation of Christ by Thomas a Kempis

Homage to Catalonia by George Orwell

The Evolution of Civilizations: An Introduction to Historical Analysis by Carroll Quigley

Moral Man and Immoral Society: A Study in Ethics and Politics by Reinhold Niebuhr

The Confessions of Nat Turner by William Styron

Politics as a Vocation by Max Weber

You Can't Go Home Again by Thomas Wolfe

Nonzero: The Logic of Human Destiny by Robert Wright

The Collected Poems of W. B. Yeats by William Butler Yeats

index

From Advanced Sudoku to Zulu, you'll find everything you need in the **teach yourself** range, in books, on CD and on DVD.

Visit **www.teachyourself.co.uk** for more details.

Advanced Sudoku and Kakuro	Beginner's French
Afrikaans	Beginner's German
Alexander Technique	Beginner's Greek
Algebra	Beginner's Greek Script
Ancient Greek	Beginner's Hindi
Applied Psychology	Beginner's Hindi Script
Arabic	Beginner's Italian
Arabic Conversation	Beginner's Japanese
Aromatherapy	Beginner's Japanese Script
Art History	Beginner's Latin
Astrology	Beginner's Mandarin Chinese
Astronomy	Beginner's Portuguese
AutoCAD 2004	Beginner's Russian
AutoCAD 2007	Beginner's Russian Script
Ayurveda	Beginner's Spanish
Baby Massage and Yoga	Beginner's Turkish
Baby Signing	Beginner's Urdu Script
Baby Sleep	Bengali
Bach Flower Remedies	Better Bridge
Backgammon	Better Chess
Ballroom Dancing	Better Driving
Basic Accounting	Better Handwriting
Basic Computer Skills	Biblical Hebrew
Basic Mathematics	Biology
Beauty	Birdwatching
Beekeeping	Blogging
Beginner's Arabic Script	Body Language
Beginner's Chinese Script	Book Keeping
Beginner's Dutch	Brazilian Portuguese

Bridge
British Citizenship Test, The
British Empire, The
British Monarchy from Henry
   VIII, The
Buddhism
Bulgarian
Bulgarian Conversation
Business French
Business Plans
Business Spanish
Business Studies
C++
Calculus
Calligraphy
Cantonese
Caravanning
Car Buying and Maintenance
Card Games
Catalan
Chess
Chi Kung
Chinese Medicine
Christianity
Classical Music
Coaching
Cold War, The
Collecting
Computing for the Over 50s
Consulting
Copywriting
Correct English
Counselling
Creative Writing
Cricket
Croatian
Crystal Healing
CVs
Czech
Danish
Decluttering
Desktop Publishing
Detox
Digital Home Movie Making
Digital Photography
Dog Training
Drawing

Dream Interpretation
Dutch
Dutch Conversation
Dutch Dictionary
Dutch Grammar
Eastern Philosophy
Electronics
English as a Foreign Language
English Grammar
English Grammar as a Foreign
   Language
Entrepreneurship
Estonian
Ethics
Excel 2003
Feng Shui
Film Making
Film Studies
Finance for Non-Financial
   Managers
Finnish
First World War, The
Fitness
Flash 8
Flash MX
Flexible Working
Flirting
Flower Arranging
Franchising
French
French Conversation
French Dictionary
French for Homebuyers
French Grammar
French Phrasebook
French Starter Kit
French Verbs
French Vocabulary
Freud
Gaelic
Gaelic Conversation
Gaelic Dictionary
Gardening
Genetics
Geology
German
German Conversation

German Grammar
German Phrasebook
German Starter Kit
German Vocabulary
Globalization
Go
Golf
Good Study Skills
Great Sex
Green Parenting
Greek
Greek Conversation
Greek Phrasebook
Growing Your Business
Guitar
Gulf Arabic
Hand Reflexology
Hausa
Herbal Medicine
Hieroglyphics
Hindi
Hindi Conversation
Hinduism
History of Ireland, The
Home PC Maintenance and
  Networking
How to DJ
How to Run a Marathon
How to Win at Casino Games
How to Win at Horse Racing
How to Win at Online Gambling
How to Win at Poker
How to Write a Blockbuster
Human Anatomy & Physiology
Hungarian
Icelandic
Improve Your French
Improve Your German
Improve Your Italian
Improve Your Spanish
Improving Your Employability
Indian Head Massage
Indonesian
Instant French
Instant German
Instant Greek
Instant Italian

Instant Japanese
Instant Portuguese
Instant Russian
Instant Spanish
Internet, The
Irish
Irish Conversation
Irish Grammar
Islam
Israeli-Palestinian Conflict, The
Italian
Italian Conversation
Italian for Homebuyers
Italian Grammar
Italian Phrasebook
Italian Starter Kit
Italian Verbs
Italian Vocabulary
Japanese
Japanese Conversation
Java
JavaScript
Jazz
Jewellery Making
Judaism
Jung
Kama Sutra, The
Keeping Aquarium Fish
Keeping Pigs
Keeping Poultry
Keeping a Rabbit
Knitting
Korean
Latin
Latin American Spanish
Latin Dictionary
Latin Grammar
Letter Writing Skills
Life at 50: For Men
Life at 50: For Women
Life Coaching
Linguistics
LINUX
Lithuanian
Magic
Mahjong
Malay

Managing Stress
Managing Your Own Career
Mandarin Chinese
Mandarin Chinese Conversation
Marketing
Marx
Massage
Mathematics
Meditation
Middle East Since 1945, The
Modern China
Modern Hebrew
Modern Persian
Mosaics
Music Theory
Mussolini's Italy
Nazi Germany
Negotiating
Nepali
New Testament Greek
NLP
Norwegian
Norwegian Conversation
Old English
One-Day French
One-Day French – the DVD
One-Day German
One-Day Greek
One-Day Italian
One-Day Polish
One-Day Portuguese
One-Day Spanish
One-Day Spanish – the DVD
One-Day Turkish
Origami
Owning a Cat
Owning a Horse
Panjabi
PC Networking for Small Businesses
Personal Safety and Self Defence
Philosophy
Philosophy of Mind
Philosophy of Religion
Phone French
Phone German

Phone Italian
Phone Japanese
Phone Mandarin Chinese
Phone Spanish
Photography
Photoshop
PHP with MySQL
Physics
Piano
Pilates
Planning Your Wedding
Polish
Polish Conversation
Politics
Portuguese
Portuguese Conversation
Portuguese for Homebuyers
Portuguese Grammar
Portuguese Phrasebook
Postmodernism
Pottery
PowerPoint 2003
PR
Project Management
Psychology
Quick Fix French Grammar
Quick Fix German Grammar
Quick Fix Italian Grammar
Quick Fix Spanish Grammar
Quick Fix: Access 2002
Quick Fix: Excel 2000
Quick Fix: Excel 2002
Quick Fix: HTML
Quick Fix: Windows XP
Quick Fix: Word
Quilting
Recruitment
Reflexology
Reiki
Relaxation
Retaining Staff
Romanian
Running Your Own Business
Russian
Russian Conversation
Russian Grammar
Sage Line 50

Sanskrit
Screenwriting
Second World War, The
Serbian
Setting Up a Small Business
Shorthand Pitman 2000
Sikhism
Singing
Slovene
Small Business Accounting
Small Business Health Check
Songwriting
Spanish
Spanish Conversation
Spanish Dictionary
Spanish for Homebuyers
Spanish Grammar
Spanish Phrasebook
Spanish Starter Kit
Spanish Verbs
Spanish Vocabulary
Speaking On Special Occasions
Speed Reading
Stalin's Russia
Stand Up Comedy
Statistics
Stop Smoking
Sudoku
Swahili
Swahili Dictionary
Swedish
Swedish Conversation
Tagalog
Tai Chi
Tantric Sex
Tap Dancing
Teaching English as a Foreign
    Language
Teams & Team Working
Thai
Thai Conversation
Theatre
Time Management
Tracing Your Family History
Training
Travel Writing
Trigonometry

Turkish
Turkish Conversation
Twentieth Century USA
Typing
Ukrainian
Understanding Tax for Small
    Businesses
Understanding Terrorism
Urdu
Vietnamese
Visual Basic
Volcanoes, Earthquakes and
    Tsunamis
Watercolour Painting
Weight Control through Diet &
    Exercise
Welsh
Welsh Conversation
Welsh Dictionary
Welsh Grammar
Wills & Probate
Windows XP
Wine Tasting
Winning at Job Interviews
Word 2003
World Faiths
Writing Crime Fiction
Writing for Children
Writing for Magazines
Writing a Novel
Writing a Play
Writing Poetry
Xhosa
Yiddish
Yoga
Your Wedding
Zen
Zulu